W9-AGA-573

The Art of Tahiti
and the neighbouring Society, Austral and Cook Islands

Terence Barrow

THAMES AND HUDSON

In memory of Roger Duff

Any copy of this book issued by the publisher as a paperback is sold subject to the condition that it shall not, by way of trade or otherwise, be lent, re-sold, hired out or otherwise circulated, without the publisher's prior consent, in any form of binding or cover other than that in which it is published, and without a similar condition including these words being imposed on a subsequent purchaser.

© Blacker Calmann Cooper Ltd, 1979
This book was designed and produced by
Blacker Calmann Cooper Ltd, London

All rights reserved. No part of this publication may be reproduced or transmitted in any form or by any means, electronic or mechanical, including photocopy, recording or any information storage and retrieval system, without permission in writing from the publishers.

Filmset by Southern Positives and Negatives (SPAN), Lingfield, Surrey
Printed in Spain by Heraclio Fournier, S.A.

Library of Congress Catalog card number: 79-63810

Contents

Introduction

Images of the gods, the regalia of divine chiefs, ornaments, adzes, fishhooks, and fallen temples—the vestiges and fragments of South Sea civilizations—have fascinated Western man since European adventurers first penetrated the South Pacific. The vision of Tahiti as an island paradise is at the heart of much of the romantic feeling about the islands of the Pacific. This emotional attachment to Tahiti has endured for over two centuries but the nature of Tahitian arts and the facts of Tahitian life remain obscure. This book is published in the hope that the veil will be lifted a little more. Of course the transient world of Tahitian song, dance, ritual and domestic life is virtually lost to us. The descriptive journals of explorers and missionaries, the artifacts they collected, and their records of native lore, are all that remains of a past destroyed by time and vandalism.

The sad devastation of Polynesian populations by foreign diseases to which they had no immunity and then through exploitation by Europeans, reduced indigenous communities to such a poor state that their arts and traditions wilted away. The Christian missionaries who followed in the wake of the explorers came with the best intentions but were the declared enemies of traditional Polynesian religion and its images. Their converts tore down temples and burned the so-called 'idols' with enthusiasm. Then came the motley band of whalers, sandalwood traders, merchants, blackbirders and beachcombers who were only concerned to exploit the natural resources of the islands, and who were indifferent to the traditional culture. In view of the facts of Pacific history, the indigenous Polynesians were lucky to survive in sufficient numbers to renew their societies by increasing their population to its present healthy level. The traditional arts were less fortunate. Such objects that have survived were those collected by early visitors.

Traditional Polynesian art was cut short by the impact of a much more developed technological society. The old craftsmen based their work on a stone-age technology set in a precarious economy which of necessity relied on horticulture, primitive animal husbandry (dog, pig and jungle fowl), and the products of the sea. Just as the technology of the South-Sea stone age is evident in the materials—wood, stone, bone and shell—used in the art, so the ideas of South-Sea man are revealed in its images. Tribal life was based on beliefs in the power of gods and spirits, the dominant subject-matter of the art.

Polynesian art also reflects the courage and enterprise of a sea people who ventured out on a trackless sea to establish new communities on remote islands. Four primary artifacts—the canoe,

1. A tattooed chief of Rarotonga in the Cook Islands, identified as 'Te Po' (correctly, probably, Te Pou, meaning 'the post'). The curious tattoo pattern, with turtle symbols on the knees, is not known from other records, although similar headdresses (plate 82) and fans exist in collections of Cook Island art. The print by G. Baxter, after a painting by J. Williams Jr., was published in London in 1837.

2. A watercolour drawing of a Tahitian double canoe made in 1777 by John Webber, the artist on HMS *Resolution*. This is a classic study of a general voyaging canoe of intermediate size, clearly showing its decorative carvings. The hull is built on a dugout with planks which are stitched together with coconut-fibre sennit. *London, British Library*

adze, fishhook and cordage—made possible the settlement of the islands and thereafter sustained the new communities. Other items were important, for example the ubiquitous bark cloth which had many uses in religious and domestic life, but none compared in importance with these four. It is generally among these primary artifacts that a singular beauty of sculptural form can be found. They mostly served a humble role as everyday tools of work and are generally undecorated. All of them, however, including cordage, had more elaborate, ritual forms which are highly ornamental. In any book dealing with arts the ritual objects tend to get pride of place as indeed they do in this book, but it is perhaps the undecorated objects that are more revealing of the aesthetic values of the community.

Tahiti is the largest of the Society Islands, which with the Cook and Austral Islands, form a cultural unit of three more or less closely related archipelagoes in Eastern Polynesia. They are at the heart of the so-called Polynesian triangle, which has sides of about 4,000 miles with corners at Hawaii, New Zealand, and Easter

3. Matavai Bay in Tahiti painted in 1773 by William Hodges, the artist on Captain Cook's second voyage. Cook's ships HMS *Resolution* and HMS *Adventure* are in the background and there are Tahitian canoes in the foreground. Much of what we know about ancient Polynesia derives from the written records of Cook and his men who charted numerous known and unknown Pacific islands. Tahiti served as a centre for the early Western voyagers in Polynesia because of the excellent natural harbour at Matavai Bay. *Greenwich, National Maritime Museum*

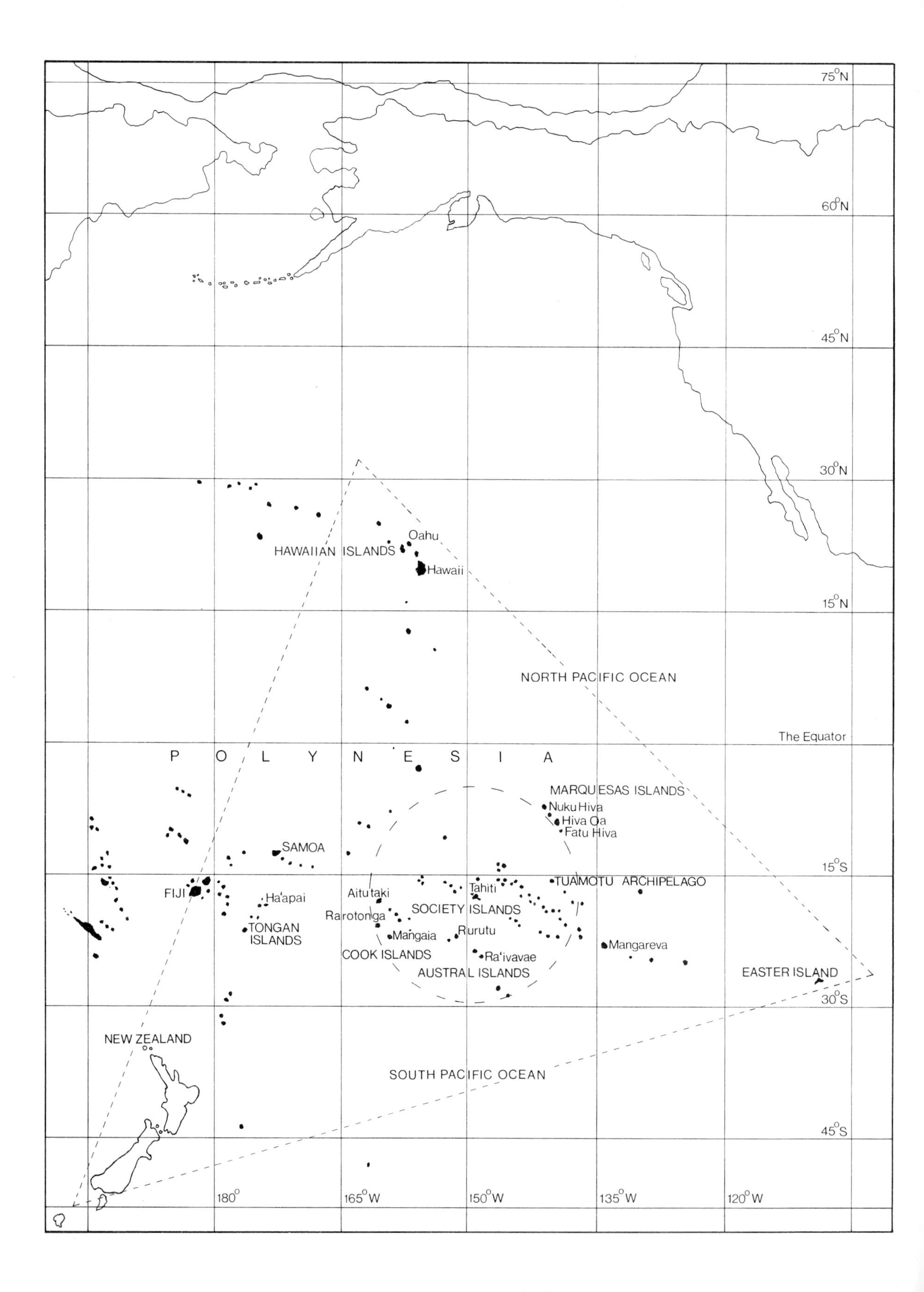
75°N
60°N
45°N
30°N
15°N
The Equator
15°S
30°S
45°S
180°
165°W
150°W
135°W
120°W
HAWAIIAN ISLANDS
Oahu
Hawaii
NORTH PACIFIC OCEAN
P O L Y N E S I A
MARQUESAS ISLANDS
Nuku Hiva
Hiva Oa
Fatu Hiva
SAMOA
FIJI
Ha'apai
TONGAN ISLANDS
Aitutaki
Rarotonga
Tahiti
SOCIETY ISLANDS
TUAMOTU ARCHIPELAGO
Mangaia
Rurutu
COOK ISLANDS
Ra'ivavae
AUSTRAL ISLANDS
Mangareva
EASTER ISLAND
NEW ZEALAND
SOUTH PACIFIC OCEAN

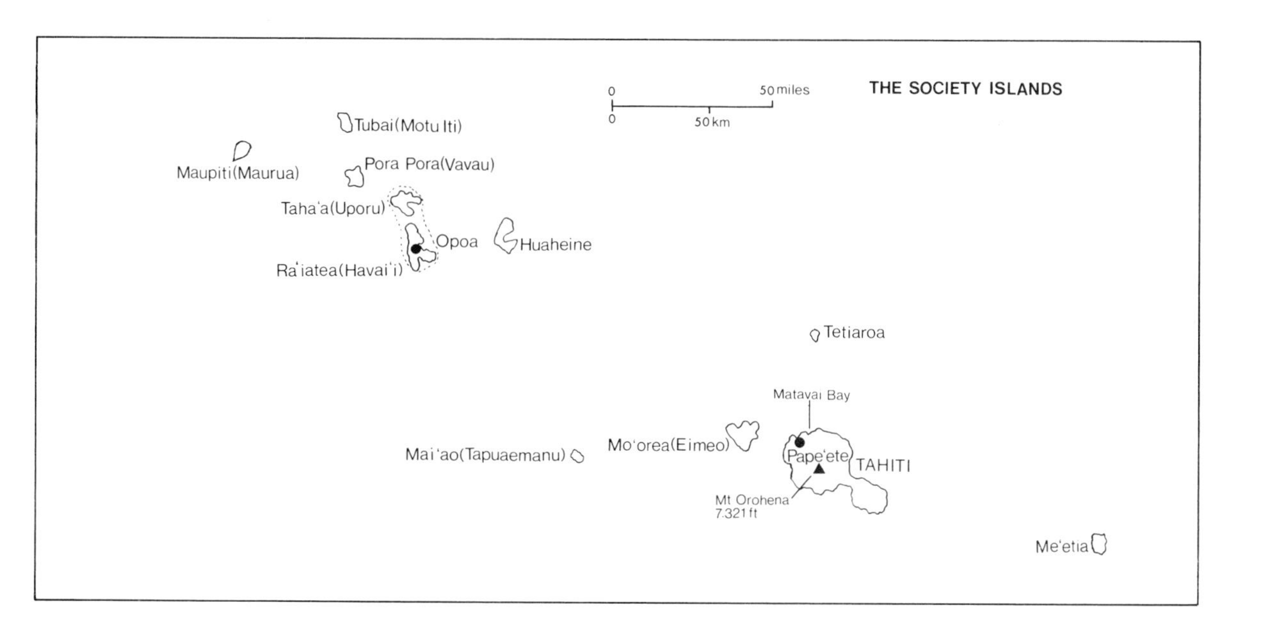

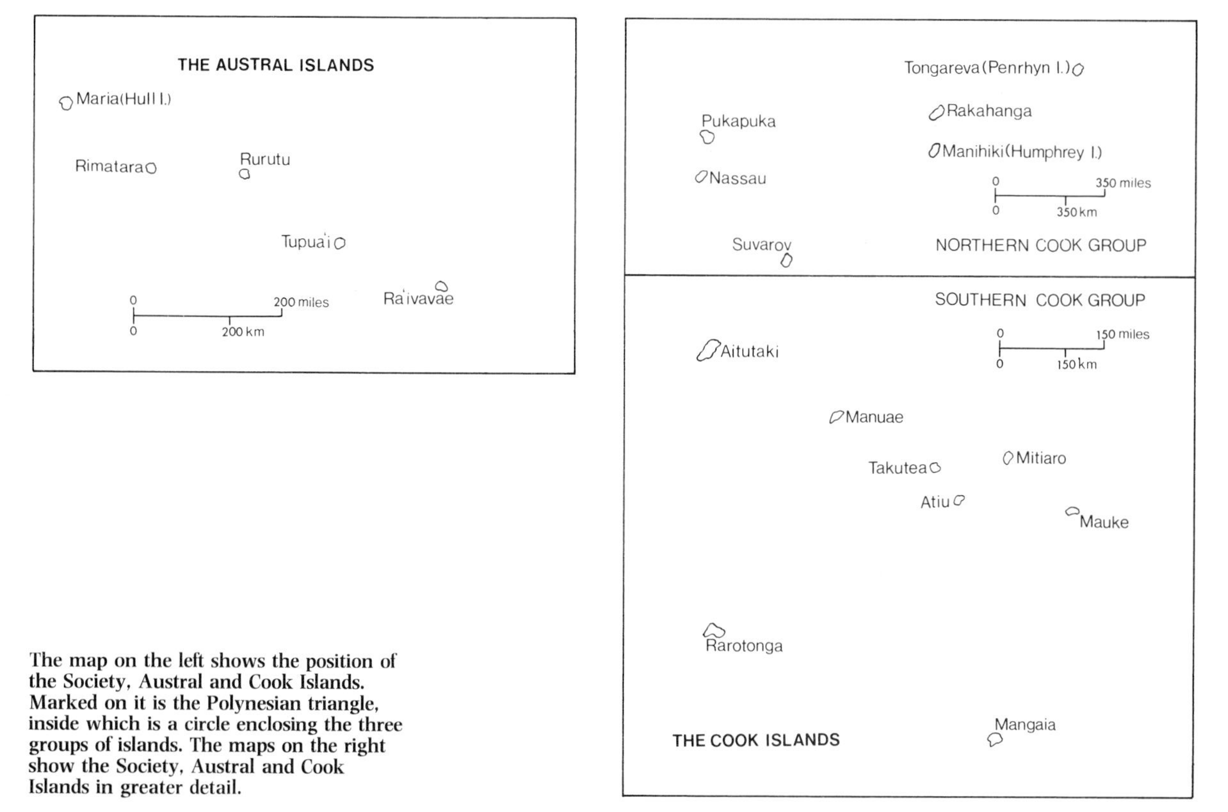

The map on the left shows the position of the Society, Austral and Cook Islands. Marked on it is the Polynesian triangle, inside which is a circle enclosing the three groups of islands. The maps on the right show the Society, Austral and Cook Islands in greater detail.

4. A wash drawing of Matavai Bay in 1774 by William Hodges. The carved columns set on the upswept stern of the canoe on the right indicate the use of images. *London, British Museum*

Island. Tahiti is the geographic centre of the triangle as can be seen on the map. It is also at the heart of the Society-Cook-Austral complex of islands. To see this one can draw a circle with Tahiti as its centre and Rarotonga as a point on the circumference. All the islands within the circle are those with whose art we are concerned in this book, with the exception of the Tuamotuan Archipelago which produced little sculptural art. The Marquesas, from where the ancestors of the Tahitians are supposed to have come, are just beyond the perimeter to the northwest.

The islands in the Polynesian area, with the exception of New Zealand and Hawaii, are mere specks of land when viewed as part of the Pacific, yet they were found and inhabited by settlers who arrived well over a thousand years ago.

The method and pattern of the settlement of Polynesia is now more or less understood. The ancestors of the Polynesians occupied regions in East Indonesia, coastal Southeast Asia, and the Philippine Islands. These peoples, the Malayo-Polynesians or Proto-Polynesians, were speakers of the widespread Austronesian language. They were descended from the neolithic people who, as horticulturalists and fishermen, had occupied the Southeast Asian region for five or six thousand years before the time of Christ. These people became sufficiently skilled as canoe builders and navigators to go on exploratory voyages looking for new islands, guided only by the sun, clouds, winds, stars and birds, and by the tides and swell of the sea itself.

The geographical movements of the ancestors of the Polynesians can in part be traced through the excavation of sites, which yield earthenware of the so-called Lapita sea-nomads who flourished from 1500-500 BC. The Lapita pottery sherds reveal a trail which leads from the coasts of New Guinea to Fiji, Tonga and Samoa in West Polynesia, where it seems they were entrenched well before 1000 BC. It was there that their culture developed into the form we know as Polynesian before being carried east in fine voyaging canoes in a constant quest for new island homes. Pottery has been found in the Marquesas Islands indicating a settlement there a century or so before the Christian era. Within a few centuries, near and distant islands were populated from the Marquesas Islands, including the Society Islands, Hawaii, New Zealand and Easter

5. A pencil and watercolour sketch of a man of Rurutu, one of the Austral Islands, by John Webber. This skilful portrait shows the tattoo patterns of the people of Rurutu and matches the description in Joseph Banks's journal, written during his visit to the island with HMS *Endeavour* in 1769. John Webber never visited Rurutu, so he must have met and sketched this Rurutuan in the Society Islands. *London, British Library*

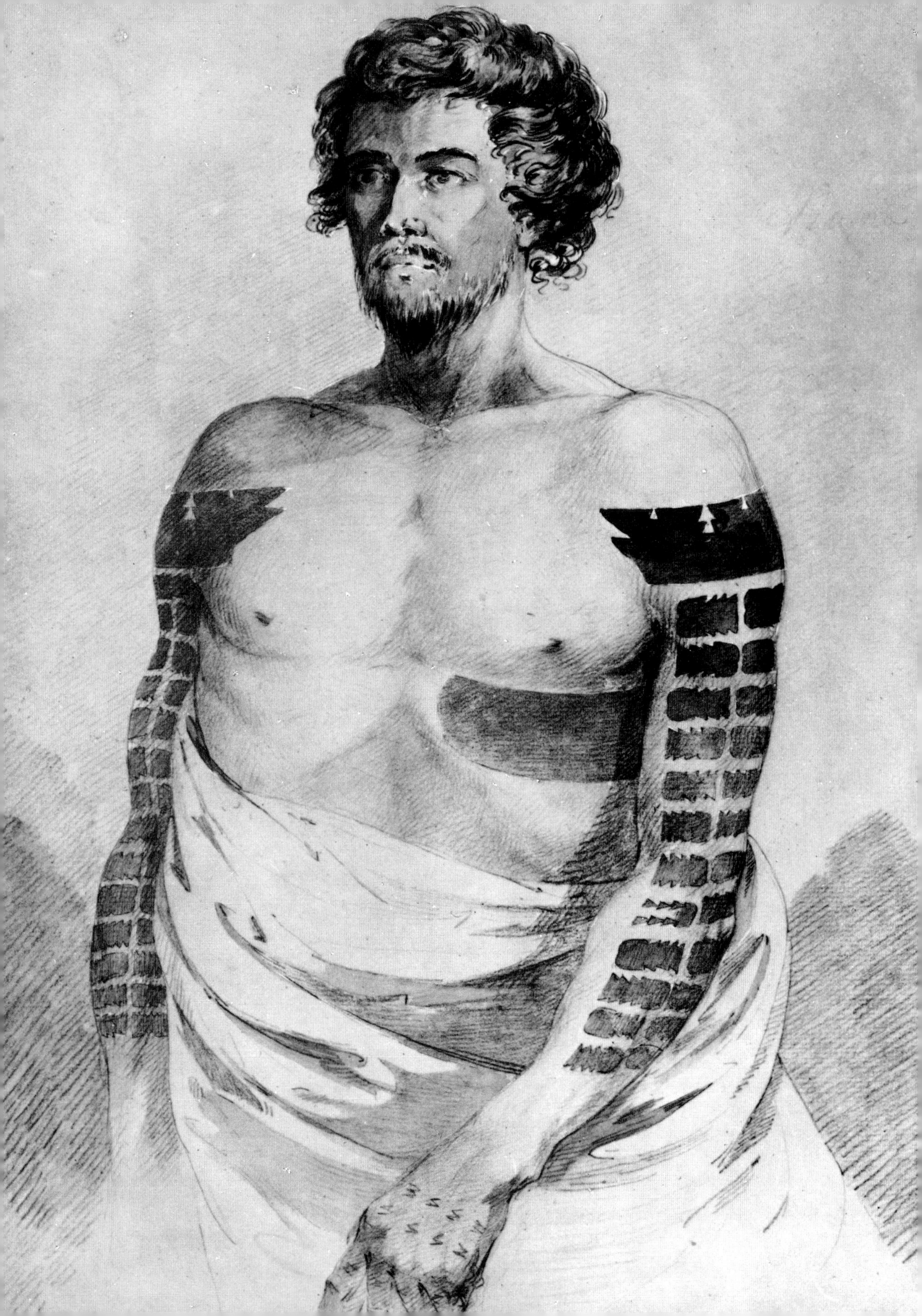

Island. The Society Islands were settled at some time around the seventh or eighth centuries, and the communities there developed at leisure for over a thousand years before the fatal appearance of Western man.

There were great refinements in Polynesian culture, supporting the idea that elements from the older civilizations of India and China were in fact carried to this island world by the aboriginal settlers. The classic chiefdoms, which Europeans described in the late eighteenth century, exhibit a more or less rigid class structure. A high aristocracy, headed by divine chiefs with their attendant priests, ruled over a subservient multitude. Massive stone temples, human sacrifice, and the glorification of ruling chiefs were common features of East Polynesian life except where the poverty of the environment prevented such prodigal expenditure of resources. The surpluses required to support such a system of lavish display and aristocratic privilege laid a weight on the economy which seems, in Tahiti for example, to have reached a critical state by the time of the first European contact; and there are reasons to believe that Polynesian culture, by then, was already past its full flowering.

The Polynesians did not have clear ideas about worlds beyond their own island archipelagoes. They recalled distant homelands, but in practice identified with single islands or groups of neighbouring islands. The Tahitians, who called themselves 'Maohi', saw themselves as inhabitants of the Tahitian archipelago rather than as occupants of any one island. Mr Morrison, boatswain's mate on HMS *Bounty*, wrote:

'. . . the Inhabitants of all the Society Islands are one and the same people—Taheite is by Much the largest and most powerful when the Strength of the Island is united, and is therefore acknowledged Mistress Paramount of the whole. They all distinguish their Language, Customs, &c. by the Name of Taheite as well at home as when they are at Taheite and there are but few men of property who do not visit Taheite once in their life time and many visit it frequently.'

This is an important point, and in this present book the terms 'Tahiti' and 'Tahitian' are used in this general sense also. Where the specific island of Tahiti is referred to, this will be made clear by the context.

Another important aspect of understanding Tahitian and other Polynesian art forms is the environment. Island environments vary, and each profoundly influenced society and art. Raw materials, food supply and the socio-religious system naturally either favoured or limited art production. Only the richest islands could provide the

6. An interior view of the temple at Atahuru, Tahiti, in the year 1777. Captain Cook and some officers are shown on the right. This ghastly scene of a human sacrifice, the accumulated skulls, and offerings of dogs and hogs on the raised platforms, provides us with a glimpse of the savage side of Polynesia. The drums beaten by the men on the left are imports from the Austral Islands (plate 69).
London, British Museum

considerable surpluses necessary to support highly specialized craftsmen and a largely idle aristocracy.

There are three island types in East Polynesia, each with its own environment and productivity potential. The 'high islands' are formed from basaltic peaks rising above the sea (for example Tahiti, Ra'iatea and Rarotonga) and were highly productive. It was on these islands that classical Polynesian culture reached perfection, and the great wood and stone sculptural traditions are associated with them. In contrast we have the 'low island' or coral atoll (the Tuamotuan islands are typical) where rainfall is poor, the land of limited productivity, with the menace of hurricane and hunger a constant threat to the lives of the atoll inhabitants.

The third, or 'intermediate' type, called *makatea*, was formed when an atoll was pushed up by subterranean mountain movements, creating islands two or three hundred feet high. The former lagoons of such raised islands became basins which, over thousands or even millions of years, developed soils suitable for horticulture. Islands of this sort, such as Mangaia in the Cook Islands, were very productive centres of sculpture.

The intricacies of East Polynesian life—the *kava*-drinking ceremonies, the wide range of food-plants, the pastimes such as archery, the technology of canoe building and other such ethnographic subjects—are of necessity treated lightly in the pages that follow. We must remember, however, that tribal warfare was a constant feature of life in ancient Polynesia. The only peace was at best an armed truce; and cruel practices such as human sacrifice were considered necessary to placate the gods. The art, in its ornamental and decorative aspects, of necessity first met the requirements of the priestly religion and the tribal aristocracy. Polynesian art was no more democratic than Polynesian life. Women or outcasts who approached men engaged in sacred work, or even gazed at a sacred object, were risking their lives.

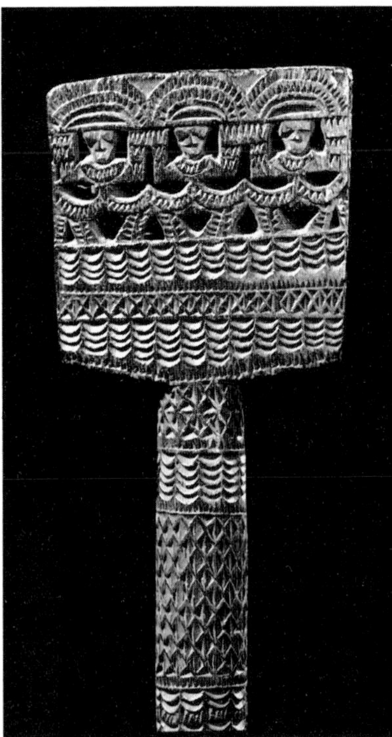

Of fundamental importance to art production was the prevailing belief in *mana*, that sacred essence of things which was believed to increase with success and decline with failure; this process applied to humans, man-made things and even to nature itself. Everything had some degree of *mana*. *Mana*'s counterpart, *tapu* (taboo in English, from the Polynesian word), is the prohibitive or protective aspect of *mana*. It was firmly believed, as indeed it was throughout much of Asia, that men represented the positive and sacred aspect of creation and as such were more *tapu* than women who expressed the profane side of the world. Women were *noa* or 'non-sacred',

7. *(Far left)* **When Captain Samuel Wallis anchored in Matavai Bay in June 1767 after his discovery of Tahiti, his crew entered into trade with the Tahitians. No one on the ship understood the Tahitian language; the first successful communication of ideas was when Wallis's sailors crowed like cocks while pointing to the shore. This acting was immediately understood. Trade proceeded peacefully until the Tahitians suddenly attacked the ships, hurling stones at the crew. This engraving depicts the Tahitian attack and the English firing their cannons in defence. The engraving is after the plate in Hawkesworth's book on Captain Cook's first Pacific voyage (1777), and is entitled 'A Representation of the ATTACK on CAPTAIN WALLIS in the DOLPHIN, by the Natives of OTAHEITE'.**

8. *(Left)* **This engraving shows a more peaceful aspect of Captain Wallis's visit to Tahiti than plate 7. It is said to depict the 'surrender of the island of Otaheite' to Captain Wallis by Purea, a female chief who the English thought was queen of all the island. The palm frond in the hand of the lady, a symbol of peace, is being offered to Captain Wallis who advances with his officers and marines. In the background is one of the great communal houses of old Tahiti. This engraving is from Hawkesworth (1777).**

9. **Detail from the top of a paddle from Ra'ivavai, one of the Austral Islands, carved in the nineteenth century. It has some of the distinctive qualities of East Polynesian art, namely an extraordinary craft skill, and great precision and delicacy of feeling.** *Cambridge, Museum of Archaeology and Ethnology*

and for this reason were forbidden to practise religious arts, eat certain foods reserved for men, or even to share meals with men. Such ideas sustained the old Polynesian world before Christianity dethroned its gods, the *tapu* prohibitions, and the very *mana* of Polynesian man. When the old beliefs were abolished the order of traditional society quite naturally fell apart, and the art died.

Ethnologists who study Polynesian art are aware, or should be aware, that they are only viewing a minute fraction of the objects that actually existed at the time of Western contact. A picture has to be built up only from fragments of the original culture. Equally important is the fact that nearly all the objects that have survived were collected over a very limited period. Miscellaneous ancient materials are found in archaeological excavations, but for all practical purposes observations on Polynesian art are based on the works collected during the few decades between the arrival of Europeans and the demise of traditional art.

Even before the extinction of traditional crafts, the use of iron tools as a substitute for stone ones very rapidly transformed the technical side of carving. Barrel-hoop iron, for example, made good adze blades while ships' nails were easily converted into chisels and drills. Such tools encouraged carvers to work more rapidly and on a grander scale, which resulted in a temporary 'efflorescence' of the traditional carving art. The earliest carvings made with metal tools are not easily distinguishable from stone-tool work, yet changes in style become increasingly obvious. To meet the requirements of visitors, carving grew increasingly less restrained and more spectacular: Ra'ivavaean drum bases, Austral paddles and Mangaian adzes provide excellent examples of this changing and decadent style. This 'souvenir' art, however, did not long survive, and with it perished what remained of the ancient sculptural tradition.

The decline of traditional Tahitian art can be conveniently dated to 1767, the year the British seaman Captain Wallis discovered Tahiti. Its convenient situation, its obliging, charming people, clear water, and the harbour at Matavai Bay, made it an ideal base for Pacific explorations. Captain James Cook, the greatest of the Pacific maritime explorers, visited Tahiti on his three voyages in 1769, 1773 and 1777. Thereafter the convergence of British, French and Spanish vessels on Tahiti was so intensive that Tahitian life changed rapidly. William Bligh, who visited Tahiti in 1777 as Captain Cook's sailing master on HMS *Resolution*, returned as commander of HMS *Bounty* in search of breadfruit trees in 1788. He commented on the great changes for the worse on the island. Old customs had been abandoned, houses he had

10. A portrait of Omai, who originally came from the island of Ulaiatea. Omai was taken from the Society Islands to England on the HMS *Resolution* in 1773. He was given the status of an ordinary seaman so that he could draw pay. He was patronized by the First Lord of the Admiralty, the Earl of Sandwich, and remained under the personal care of Sir Joseph Banks. When he was presented to King George III, he forgot his carefully rehearsed lines, and improvised with, 'Howdo! King Tosh!' which delighted the king. Later on in a speech to King George, he said, 'Sir, you are King of England, Tahiti, Ulaiatea and Pora pora—as your subject I am here to get gunpowder to destroy your enemies who are the people of Pora pora.' He did not get the firearms, but was returned home with farm equipment on the HMS *Resolution*. Here Omai is clad in white bark-cloth robes and carries a Tahitian wooden seat, a symbol of his rank. This is an engraving by Bertolozzi, published in 1775, after a painting by Nathaniel Dance Holland.

known were destroyed, and an apathetic attitude to life prevailed among the Tahitians. Metal blades had replaced the old bone and stone tools, and fine craft work could no longer be obtained. The once thriving community of Tahiti was deteriorating.

On 4 March 1797, the *Duff* under Captain Wilson arrived with members of the London Missionary Society. Soon native conversion to Christianity was virtually complete and the old Tahitian religion was no more. King Pomare I's acceptance of Christianity marks the end of the old era. Most of the temples and images were destroyed by the converted Tahitians and the island was virtually denuded of its magnificent aboriginal art.

The Christian missionaries who came to the Society, Cook and Austral Islands, like their colleagues elsewhere, were a brave band of men and women, who went to Polynesia with the best intentions. Unfortunately their theology was narrow and they viewed the traditional culture as something to be destroyed as quickly as possible. Their interest in Polynesian art sprang from the habit of collecting trophies of victories over 'paganism'. When temples were being pulled down and wooden images of gods burnt by enthusiastic native converts, some objects were saved to be sent back to England. In this way, some of the finest East Polynesian art objects, including some illustrated in this book, have survived.

11 and 12. Two views of the Taputapuatea *marae* at Opoa on the sacred island of Ra'iatea. This temple, sometimes referred to as the 'International Temple' of the Tahitian islands, is the site of the original 'Oro worship. With the spread of the cult of the god 'Oro a number of temples on other Society islands were named Taputapuatea after this one. Many human sacrifices, fire-walking, and other strange religious practices would have taken place here.

13 and 14. Companion pictures from *Life in the Southern Isles*, written by the Rev. W. W. Gill and published in London, 1876. These illustrations were intended to show Polynesian life before and after 'civilization' by missionaries. This particular scene is on the island of Pukapuka in the Northern Cook Islands. The upper view shows the natives indulging in pre-Christian pagan rites, while the second presents that of an 'English' village, all peace and industry. Propaganda such as this helped raise funds in Britain and America to advance missionary work.

A remarkable example of the escape of some of the finest Cook Island staff gods is described by the Rev. John Williams in his book, *Missionary Enterprises* (London 1837). The frontispiece of the book is shown in plate 15.

'A day or two afterwards, they requested us to take our seat outside the door; and on doing so, we observed a large concourse of people coming towards us, bearing heavy burdens. They walked in procession, and dropped at our feet fourteen immense idols, the smallest of which was about five yards in length. Each of these was composed of a piece of *aito*, or iron-wood, about four inches in diameter, carved with rude imitations of the human head at one end and with an obscene figure at the other, wrapped round in native cloth, until it became two or three yards in circumference. Near the wood were red feathers and a string of small pieces of polished pearl shells, which were said to be the *manava* or soul of the god. Some of the idols were torn to pieces before our eyes; others were reserved to decorate the rafters of the chapel we

15. The people of the island of Rarotonga are seen here delivering their god images to missionaries after their conversion to Christianity. This engraving was the frontispiece of *Missionary Enterprises*, by the Rev. John Williams, published in London, 1837.

proposed to erect; and one was kept to be sent to England, which is now in the Missionary Museum.'

Missionaries' feelings of triumph at securing these works were intense. When they were sent back home and displayed, the missionaries received praise for their work which helped raise money for further enterprises. Their attitudes to Polynesians were condescending and implied a cultural inferiority which was far from the truth. But Polynesians were not easily put down. For example, a Ra'iatean carver-priest made it quite clear to the Rev. W. Ellis that he was under no delusion about the nature of his art, that he practised carving as a trade, and that the spiritual essence or power of the god *(atua)* that entered his wooden figures was due to temple ceremonial. The image representing a god, spirit or ancestor has an important place in Polynesian art, religion, and magic. But Polynesians were *not* benighted natives worshipping wooden idols. With that thought in mind, let us move on to review the arts of the Society, Cook and Austral Islands.

The Society Islands

16 and 17. Tahitian wooden figure. This battered carving, missing its arms and the forepart of the feet, remains powerfully expressive. Although we do not know what its original function was, the mood is that of a sorcerer's image rather than that of a canoe *ti'i* (page 41). The marginal illustration in black and white (plate 17) is a much earlier photograph of the same piece fitted with a Tahitian feather wreath.
Height: 25 in (63·5 cm). London, British Museum

The Society Islands run on a southeast axis, and are aligned with the path of the prevailing trade winds (see map p. 9). The southerly, or windward, group consists of Tahiti, Mo'orea, Me'etia, Mai'ao, and Tetiaroa; the leeward group is Ra'iatea, Taha'a, Huahine, Pora Pora, Tubai, and Maupiti. With the exception of Tubai and Tetiaroa, they are high-island types, well watered, with lagoons inside barrier reefs. The large, fertile land mass of Tahiti, rising to 7,321 feet in Mount Orohena, could support a large population and in time became a focal point of economic and political activity.

At the time of European discovery, it was divided into three major chiefdoms. However, a relatively minor chief, Tu, whose district included Matavai Bay where European ships anchored, gained an early advantage through contact with foreigners. The firearms and other weapons he acquired from them enabled him to bring the entire island under his domination, and he established himself as king under the name of Pomare I.

If we are to understand better the arts of Tahiti it is necessary to know something of the history of the early contacts with Europeans. It was then that most of the art objects of our study were collected and the written records of traditional Tahitian life were made.

The Tahitian scene appeared singularly idyllic to eighteenth-century visitors. The portraits of Poetua (plate 27) and the girl bearing gifts (plate 39) suggest something of the beauty of Tahitian women, while the views of tranquil bays (plate 3) and rural peace (plate 22) convey to us the serenity of ancient Tahiti. The ritual and domestic art objects have the same mood of quietness, but with an inner vitality which is far from tranquil.

The fatal impact of the West on Tahitian culture began in earnest soon after the 'discovery' of the island by Captain Samuel Wallis in June 1767. European vessels started to arrive with surprising regularity. In the next 21 years, one expedition from France, two from Spain and five from England landed at Tahiti. Amongst the English visitors was Captain Bligh of HMS *Bounty* who arrived in 1788. The *Bounty* returned in 1789, but this time under Fletcher Christian and his band of fellow mutineers. Although glamourized by novelists and Hollywood script writers at the expense of Captain Bligh, one of the truly great seafarers of the eighteenth century, the mutineers did much to destroy traditional Tahitian life through their military involvement in the island and by providing firearms for the inhabitants.

In 1797, a group of British Protestant missionaries arrived on HMS *Duff*. An earnest group of men and women, they astonished the Tahitians who were more accustomed to lecherous and rowdy

18. *(Left)* **King Pomare I, who established himself as king of Tahiti (page 21). Portrait by William Hodges.** *21¼ × 15 in (54·0 × 37·8 cm). Canberra, National Library of Australia*

19. *(Right)* **An engraving from a sketch by John Webber entitled 'A Dance in Otaheiti'. This scene is one of the most charming pictures of South-Sea life to have come down to us. It illustrates the harmonious aspect of Tahitian life. Music in old Polynesia was similar to that of classic Greece; sound, bodily movement, and words in the form of chant, were all parts of an indivisible art. Webber is known to have sketched accurately, so the costumes of the young women, made from soft bark-cloth and decorated with feathers, are probably true to life.** *London, British Library*

sailors. By 1820 conversion to Christianity was complete. Traditional religion, native craftsmanship, the Arioi performances (below), legend recitations, chants, and dance—in fact, most of what was at the core of Tahitian life and art—were suppressed. The modern era began with reading, writing, the wearing of tailored fabrics, and the use of metal tools. There was no longer a place for the *tahu'a*, the craftsmen priests of old Tahiti.

Social Structure

Tahitian society consisted of three distinct classes. At the top were the high chiefs *(ali'i)* with the upper caste of royalty at their head. The middlemen *(ra'atira)* were the backbone of society as proprietary farmers, landed gentry, warriors, and administrators. The common people *(manahune)* were the oppressed labouring lower stratum. Between the high and powerful *feia mana* and the low *te fanau'a oura ri'i*, or 'progeny of little shrimps', the gap was unpassable.

The Arioi Society existed on the periphery of the classes. Its members were travelling players devoted to entertaining all sections of the populace, and their chants and dances served to perpetuate traditions. The notoriety they enjoyed in the West derived from their canoe-wandering habits, their sexual licence, the fact that they were obliged to destroy their offspring or resign

20. Two Tahitian bamboo nose flutes. The flute on the left is bound with fine sennit made from coconut husk fibre. Both were blown with the nose through a hole at the top. *Lengths: left: 15½ in (39·5 cm); right: 16½ in (42 cm). Cambridge, Museum of Archaeology and Ethnology*

their membership, and their locust-like rapacity which desolated the districts they visited. Some Tahitians moved their homes inland to be out of reach of the Arioi. The missionaries hated their eroticism, their devotion to dance, pleasure and their god, 'Oro.

Tahitian art existed on two levels: the religious and ritualistic, and the domestic and secular. As the life of *ali'i*, *ra'atira*, and *manahune* differed at the ritualistic and economic levels, so the objects used differed in quality and type. The finest work was made by specialist experts of high social rank for the aristocracy (which included the *ra'atira* as well as the *ali'i*). Tahitian art, at its highest level, was an art of aristocrats and priestly experts. The common people managed as well as they could with their simple garments and huts, modest canoes, and a few domestic utensils. Even the humblest were not immune to the rapacity of chiefs: so any *manahune* possessing more than it was thought he deserved was deprived of his goods.

Domestic Crafts

Tahitian settlements usually consisted of scattered hamlets of scarcely more than half-a-dozen houses set among shade trees and dispersed along the coasts. Some of the inhabitants settled in valleys, although the Tahitians were essentially a coast-dwelling people devoted to fishing and, perhaps less enthusiastically, to

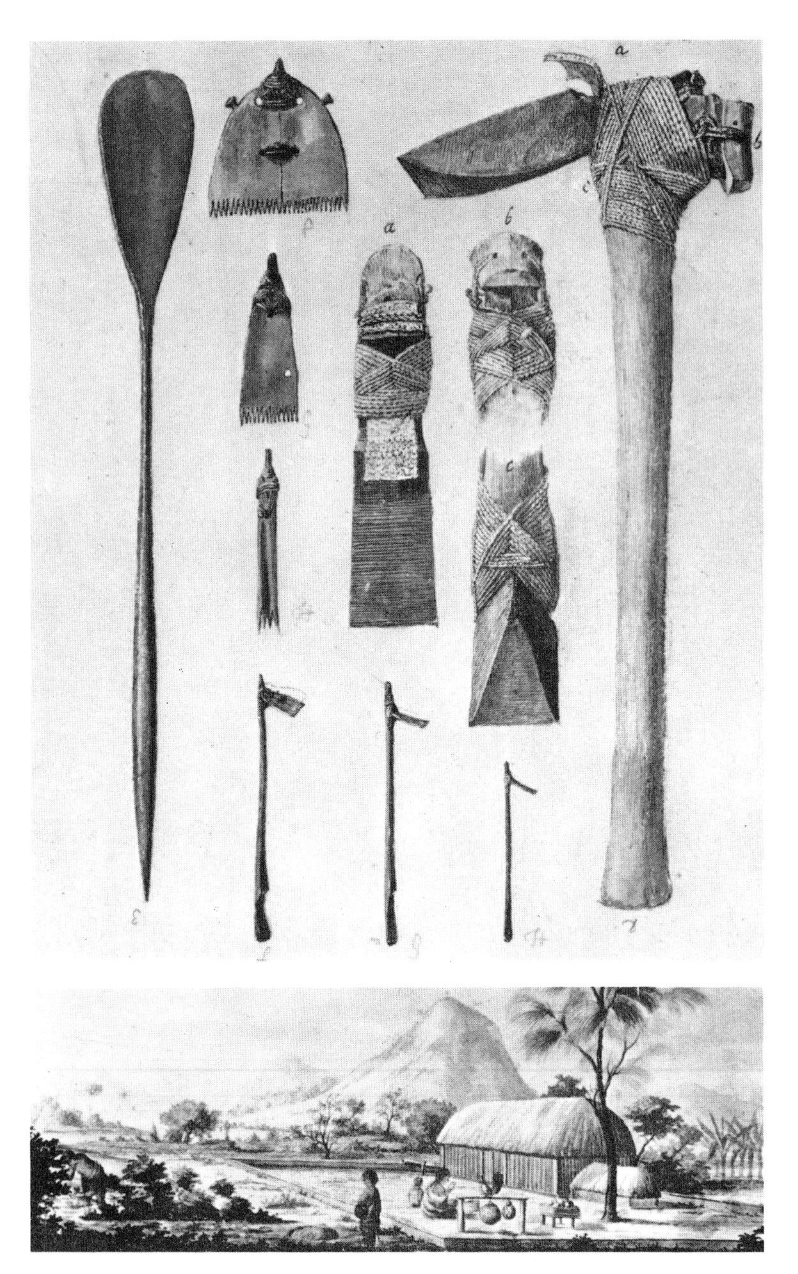

21 and 23. *(Above left and right)* Two groups of artifacts from Tahiti. The group on the left consists of a tattooing beater, three tattooing instruments seen from the side and above, and side and top view of an adze. The group on the right consists of a nose flute, a basalt food pounder, a chisel with a human-bone blade, an adze with a rotating blade and a thatching needle. From a drawing by J. F. Miller, 1771. *London, British Library*

22. The house and plantations of a chief of the island of Tahiti, drawn by Sydney Parkinson who visited Tahiti in 1769 as the artist on Captain Cook's HMS *Endeavour*. The idyllic landscape and the neatness of the Tahitian domestic scene are evident from this charming sketch. *London, British Library*

horticulture and animal husbandry. Houses were rectangular with squared or oval ends, ranging in size from the huts of the *manahune* to the fine dwellings of the *ali'i*, including great community houses measuring up to 200 feet (65 metres) in length by 30 feet (10 metres) in width. There were structures built for special purposes: storage for canoes, bark-cloth-making shelters, and cookhouses.

Household furnishings were modest, regardless of social standing. Mats, seats, headrests, stone lamps (which burnt oil from candle nuts), bark-cloth bed covers, and baskets served most domestic needs. Kitchen utensils were likewise limited. Bowls of oval form and slightly pointed at one end, stone pounders (plate 24), pounding tables, and wooden breadfruit splitters (plate 25) are

24. Three pounders used for mashing *taro* (a root vegetable) or breadfruit into the paste which was fermented into the vegetable mash *poi*. The two basalt pounders on the left are of a Tahitian type; that on the right is made of coral, a material commonly used for pounders in the Austral Islands. *Cambridge, Museum of Archaeology and Ethnology*

25. Two Tahitian hardwood breadfruit splitters. These utilitarian household implements, shaped rather like adzes, possess strong sculptural form. *Length: $12\frac{1}{4}$ in (31 cm). Cambridge, Museum of Archaeology and Ethnology*

often of such austere sculptural beauty that they truly rank as art objects. House lashing, basketry, mat-patterning, and other utilitarian crafts were extensively practised domestic arts, yet extant collections of them do not give us a complete picture of daily life.

Clothes and Tattooing

Bark-cloth *(tapa)* manufacture and decoration was a central art for women of all grades. The cloth was made by beating with mallets the soft inner layer of the bark of certain trees. Aristocratic women positively vied with each other at it, working in groups, chatting and singing above the din of beater on anvil. Its rich patterns make bark-cloth rank as the most decorative of Tahitian arts. Tahitian *tapa* does not have the stamped or lined designs commonly seen in Hawaiian and West Polynesian bark-cloth, yet it was decorated with strong patterns painted freehand in various colours, or with the impression of leaves and ferns dipped in brown pigment and then pressed on the cloth (plate 30).

Clothing and body tattoos indicated social standing by quality rather than anything else. Garments consisted simply of the male girdle or loin cloth *(maro)*, a wrap-around *pareu* waist cloth worn by both men and women, and ponchos of decorated bark-cloth (plates 26, 30, 31) or fine matting. Large toga-like cloaks were also

26. *(Right)* **Tahitian poncho with impressed fern patterns, and three hardwood bark-cloth beaters. The garment is folded as it would have been worn. Ponchos could be worn either way round, the front and the back being interchangeable.** *Bark-cloth: 58 × 52 in (147 × 132 cm); bark-cloth beaters: approximately 14 in (35·5 cm).* Collection James Hooper

27. *(Left)* **The Ra'iatean chieftainess Poetua (Poedua), daughter of Orio, painted by John Webber. Webber met Poetua (or Poedua, as her name was spelt) when the expedition visited Matavai in 1777. Poetua is seen to possess all the beauty, charm, and grace for which Tahitian women became famous. Delicate tattoo patterns mark her arms. In her right hand she holds a fly whisk, a symbol of her rank.** *Greenwich, National Maritime Museum*

30. *(Right)* **Tahitian bark-cloth robe. The patterns are made from ferns, dipped in pigment and then impressed on the cloth.** *$78\frac{1}{2} \times 90\frac{1}{2}$ in (200×230 cm). Paris, Musée de l'Homme*

31. *(Below right)* **A decorated bark-cloth sheet with fern patterns and freehand painting. The use of fern leaves dipped in pigment as a decorative device is a Tahitian technique not seen elsewhere in Polynesia.** *$47 \times 97\frac{1}{2}$ in ($117{\cdot}5 \times 228$ cm). London, British Museum*

28. *(Below left)* **A feathered crescent ornament from the Cook Islands. Crescent and disk-shaped breast ornaments were much favoured in East Polynesia. Feathered ones, such as this, have seldom survived because of their frailty.** *$10\frac{1}{4}$ in (26 cm). Cambridge, Museum of Archaeology and Ethnology*

29. *(Below)* **A necklace made from cowrie shells, threaded on sennit braid. Various kinds of shell were commonly used as ornaments through Polynesia.** *Length of shells: 11 in (28 cm). Cambridge, Museum of Archaeology and Ethnology*

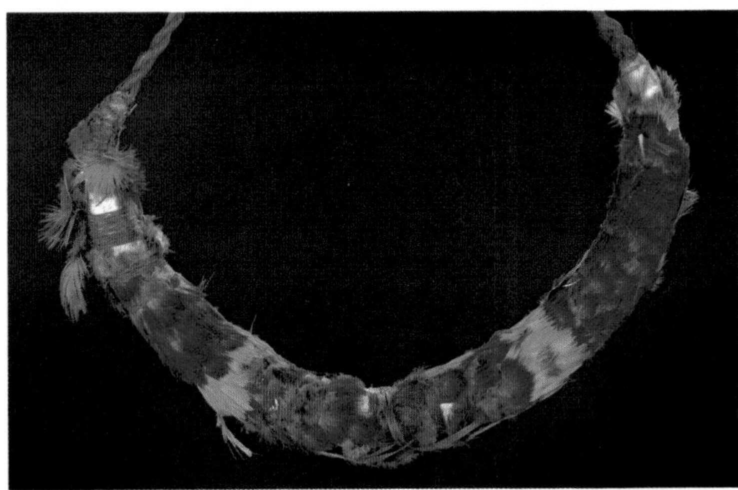

32. Chief's stool from the Cook Islands. Seats of various sizes, from small stools to the large 'thrones', were found in East Polynesia. The size and height indicated the social rank of the owner. They therefore had a ritual rather than a utilitarian function. Seats do not appear in West Polynesia, or in the marginal islands of New Zealand, Hawaii, or Easter Island. This particular seat is probably from Atiu (Cook Islands) and is a marvel of craftsmanship, cut as it is from a single block of wood. *16½ × 5¾ in (42 × 14·7 cm). Dr. R. M. Browne, Honolulu*

worn, such as that in the portrait of Omai (plate 10). Everyday headgear consisted of *tapa* turbans for men, and plaited eyeshades which women used. Women also wore earrings of shells, seeds, or pearls, but their bodily ornament other than tattoo was limited. The portraits of Omai and Poetua (plate 27) illustrate the restrained beauty of Tahitian dress.

It seems that the tattooing of men and women, apart from rank tattoos of the Arioi Society, was primarily designed to be erotic and decorative. Apart from markings on arms and legs, large areas of the buttocks were tattooed. The art was in the hands of specialists called *tahu'a tatau* who were often highly rewarded for their services. The beauties of this art are now lost to us. Unless perfect mummification could be achieved, as with the tattooed heads of New Zealand, nothing remained after a body had decomposed.

Symbols of Rank

The high ranking *ali'i* were designated by various possessions which symbolized their authority. These consisted of a wooden seat, a wooden head rest, fly whisk, helmet, spear, staff, waistband, and loin cloth of more than ordinary quality.

Feathered girdles *(maru 'ura)*, the highest symbols of temporal and divine power, were of such sanctity that human sacrifices sometimes marked stages of their manufacture. Such girdles embodied the prestige of hereditary rank, political power, and the

33. This poncho or *tiputa* from the Society Islands provides us with a good example of Tahitian freehand pattern painting on bark-cloth. The compositions vary from rigid rectangular designs, to curved shapes and a drawing of a European ship at one end. The centre hole is for the head to pass through. *68 × 22 in (173 × 65 cm). Collection George Ortiz*

territorial rights of rulers. Wars were occasionally fought over the possession of a particular girdle, while the investiture of an *ali'i* with the girdle was a highly sacred event.

A ritual loin cloth was basically a long strip of cloth about six inches wide and sometimes over twenty-one feet long with precious feathers attached to it. It was passed between the legs and wrapped around the waist several times, with the ends left to fall as a kind of drape at back and front. There were two basic types, those with red and those with yellow feathers. They were used on ceremonial occasions then returned to their storage containers.

The most unusual sacred loin cloth on record was that made for the Tahitian *ali'i* Purea, from a British flag left at Matavai Bay by Captain Wallis. It was used at the investiture of Purea's son and was later shown to Captain Cook.

Wooden seats or stools of various sizes were carved from solid blocks of ebony-like *tamanu* wood. The largest measured four or five feet in length and some three feet in height and width. Smaller Tahitian seats, such as the one held by Omai (plate 10), lacked secondary decoration. They contrast with those of the Austral Islands (plate 54). Seats were carried after a chief by retainers and sometimes distinguished guests were invited to share them. The size and degree of curvature of the top indicated the rank of the owner. There were also small head-rests resembling in form the chiefs' stools. They too were hewn from a single hard-wood block but were rarely more than nine inches wide. Some had more than four legs, while a transverse bar at the base was sometimes incorporated to give extra strength to these delicate carvings.

Although it is thought that flies were not troublesome in Polynesia until after the arrival of Europeans fly whisks were used to indicate authority both in West and East Polynesia, as they are throughout much of Asia. In Tahiti such whisks usually have a single image at the lower end of the handle or, when they are made of whale ivory, a joined and pierced handle (plate 62). Many of the more delicate fly whisks, collected in the Society Islands and labelled as 'Otaheiti', are probably of Austral Islands origin.

Canoes

Transportation by water of produce of various kinds, animals, goods, and people was vital to ordinary Tahitian economy. Ranging in size from small dugouts of ten feet to war galleys of more than a hundred feet, canoes were either single-hulled with an outrigger to give them stability, or were double-hulled. The dugouts served for fishing or local transportation and are usually seen in early

Tahitian marine scenes as, for example, in the centre on the Matavai Bay scene (plate 3). Rafts were also used but most families could afford a small dugout.

All-purpose sailing canoes, either single or double-hulled, were the work-horses of island travel (plates 2, 4). They ranged in length from twenty-five to forty feet. The high sterns were often ornamented with carvings such as we see on the *tipairua* type of vessel (plate 2). Portable shelters were set on a platform joining the hulls of the larger double canoes.

The war galleys were of two types. The *pahi*, mostly built on Ra'iatea, were deep-keeled ships made of many planks, with stages set above the hulls for the warriors to fight from. They were propelled by paddlers who did not take part in the initial fighting. Captain Cook saw a *pahi* Pomare was building which measured over 108 feet long. The King asked Captain Cook if he might name his new vessel *Britanne* (Britain) to which Cook consented, and gave 'An English Jack and Pennant' for this vessel. Some three hundred men, warriors and paddlers, would man the larger war galleys. The second type was similar to the *pahi* but had rounder hulls and fighting platforms set at the forepart of the vessel.

Naval engagements took place in sheltered waters between opposing fleets. The fleet seen by Cook and his men assembling in Tahiti for an attack on Mo'orea was composed of about one hundred and sixty war canoes and numerous support vessels (plate 37). Once battle began no quarter was given by either side. The most venerated canoes, built to carry symbols of the gods, also went to battle. They were used primarily to carry sacred relics from temple to temple, but in war at sea they acted as floating temples and were placed among the vanguard vessels, serving as rallying points when the action faltered. If they were captured, the fighting usually came to an end. Sacred canoes were sometimes left in temples or drawn ashore to serve as shrines. They were large and strong, and rituals were performed at stages of their construction. Ornamental carvings and trailing feather streamers graced these special vessels.

Ornamental carvings were extensively used on important canoes of all types. They were set on high sterns in towering pillars, with smaller carvings at the bow (plates 2, 4, 37). Anthropomorphic *ti'i* (wooden icons in human form) predominate in such decoration.

A number of craft skills merged in canoe construction. The hulls were hollowed out with stone adzes. Planks, which were made by splitting tree trunks with wedges, and then dressing them with adzes, were intricately lashed together with coconut fibre cordage

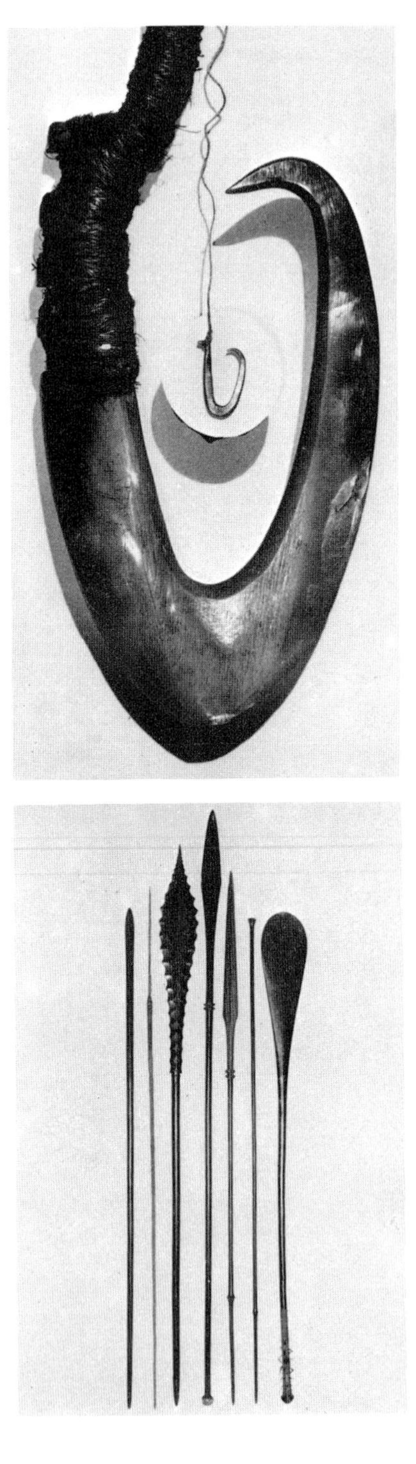

34. *(Above left)* **Two pearl-shell fishhooks used in handline fishing in Tahiti, believed to have been collected on the first voyage of Captain Cook. These hooks, both of superb form, are shown together to illustrate the great range used. Each type of fishing required a different hook; some were for handline, others for trolling or for surface fishing with a rod.** *Large hook: 6⅛ in (15 cm); small hook: ¾ in (2 cm). Cambridge, Museum of Archaeology and Ethnology*

35. *(Left)* **A group of beautifully made weapons from East Polynesia. The one second from the right would have acted as a ceremonial staff; the paddle-like artifact on the far right is a club.** *Minimum length: 96 in (244 cm). Collection James Hooper*

36. *(Above)* **Tahitian warriors in a small war canoe of** *pahi* **type, a wash drawing by Sydney Parkinson, the artist on Captain Cook's first Pacific voyage. In this study we see the dress of warriors, their weapons, the fighting canoes, and the division of crews into paddlers and fighters.** *London, British Library*

(sennit) to make the high sterns and platforms. Those working on sacred vessels were confined to sacred precincts. They were forbidden to cut their hair or to have ordinary communication with family or friends until the task was completed.

War

It appears quite clear that the ancient Tahitians indulged in war as a sport quite apart from any pressing need to protect tribal interests. Every male child was considered firstly a potential warrior. Victors in war were ruthless, often killing every man, woman, and child of the defeated faction. Destruction extended to houses, trees, and domestic animals. Loot was taken, while wholesale destruction satisfied the spirit of revenge raging in the hearts of the victors. Warfare was so intoxicating that women sometimes followed their husbands into battle, relying on stones, hands, teeth, and nails as weapons.

Hill fortresses attest to the widespread wars of former times. The main causes of conflicts were tribal rivalry, territorial claims, revenge for insults received, and the perpetuation of feuds that

37. War canoes of the *pahi* type at Pare, Tahiti, 1774, painted by William Hodges. They are shown gathering prior to an attack on Mo'orea (then known as Eimeo). Note the large headdress of the chief on the foremost canoe, and the large carved columns and fighting platform in the bow. *Greenwich, National Maritime Museum*

often endured for generations. The missionary Ellis estimated that there had been ten serious wars in the Society Islands between 1797 and 1825.

Battles were opened with the slinging or throwing of stones, which weighed from a few ounces to five pounds. As Captain Wallis and his men discovered when they were suddenly attacked in Matavai Bay, these could be very effective weapons. However Polynesians preferred to fight man-to-man with spears and clubs. They did not use shields other than paddle blades held up for protection during naval battles. The bow was known, but used only in an aristocratic sport in which archers competed for distance by shooting arrows from specially designed stone platforms.

The weapons of particular interest are the spear clubs with pointed, spatulate blades and an ornamented collar below the blades. These weapons look like spears and had pointed tops and bottoms to jab with. They were used mostly with swinging blows, so the term 'spear club' seems to describe them. Warriors showed remarkable dexterity in the mock battles observed by Europeans.

Warrior chiefs dressed in flamboyant costumes designed as much for display as for protection. They wore high headdresses (plate 38) and breast gorgets (plate 40) formed of a sennit base, with decorative feather, shark teeth, and dog hair attachments. Such dress can be seen worn by *ali'i* on the warfleet vessels (plate 37) and by a group of warriors on a small *pahi* (plate 36). Gorgets, like that on the mourner's costume in plate 51, were favourite curios. The charming girl depicted by John Webber, the artist on the HMS *Resolution*, is shown bringing gifts in the forms of lengths of bark-cloth wrapped around her body and two such gorgets (plate 39).

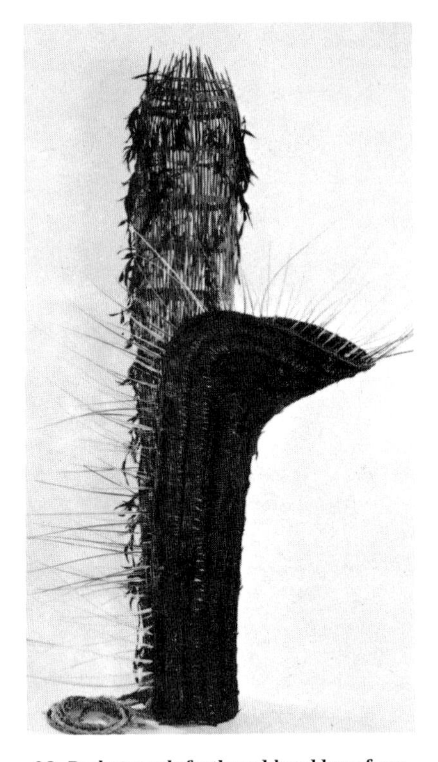

38. Basket-work feathered headdress from the Society Islands, which, with attached featherwork, stands over five feet high. Such spectacular headgear is seen worn by the commanding central figures on the war canoes in several illustrations (plates 36 and 37). *Height: 62 in (157 cm). London, British Museum*

Temples and Religious Images

Temples (plates 6, 42) were the most durable and important structures in Tahitian life. They consisted of stone work laid out in courts, terraces, and walls, with cult carvings, thatched shelters, and offering platforms arranged according to need. The 'dry wall' building of such temples called for both skill and heavy communal labour. Some were formed from terraces rising up to form a truncated pyramid, such as the famous Mahaiatea temple on Tahiti. They were the focal point of religious rituals and in them were buried the important dead, including those who had been killed as sacrifices to the gods.

Small houses or shelters near the temples were used to store all the equipment necessary for the rituals, with special houses for images of gods and for drums which played an important part in Tahitian ceremonies.

39. A Tahitian girl bearing a gift of bark-cloth and two gorgets, from a drawing by John Webber. This charming study became one of the best known Tahitian pictures, and has been redrawn and re-engraved in many versions since it was first published. At the actual event, this girl and a friend came forward, then divested themselves of their burden, leaving all behind as a gift. *London, British Library*

40. Warrior's gorget from Tahiti. Breast gorgets and high helmets, which were worn by aristocratic warriors, appear regularly in eighteenth-century pictures. The gorgets are formed on an elaborate sennit base with feathers, shark teeth, and dog hair attached to form an attractive pattern. *Width: 23 in (58·5 cm). London, British Museum*

41. Post-contact wooden *ti'i* from Mo'orea in the Society Islands. It was recently discovered with three others in a funeral cave in the valley of Opuhuna with fragments of bone. It is probably nineteenth century and was hidden at a time when *ti'i* were being burnt as a result of the conversion of the island to Christianity. *Ti'i* generally represented remote family ancestors or were the materialization of an ancestral line. *12¾ in (31 cm). Tahiti, Musée de Tahiti et des Iles*

42. **A wash drawing by Sydney Parkinson, made in 1769, of the Taputapuatea temple at Ra'iatea, with sacrificial offerings to the gods or the dead. Ra'iatea was the place of origin of 'Oro worship and acted as the spiritual centre of East Polynesia. This is one of the earliest drawings of a Tahitian temple or *marae*. The posts within the temple, which have carved birds at the top, would have long since decayed, but the stonework of many such temples remains today and has been extensively restored.** *London, British Library*

Ancient Tahitian religion centred around ritual worship of the gods and ancestral spirits. The heads of families conducted ceremonies in small temples, supplicating the spirits for help in matters of immediate local concern, such as success in an enterprise, or to secure health for an ailing kinsman. Specialist priests served in district or national temples whenever state welfare required help of the gods. There were also sorcerers, who, for a fee, manipulated spirits—the dreaded ghosts called *oromatua*—to harm enemies. In their rites they commonly used anthropomorphic carvings *(ti'i)*.

The highest *ali'i* were thought to be directly descended from the gods and were regarded as their representatives on earth; they were priests by right of this divinity. The *mana* of the gods flowed through them and for this reason the most elevated were carried on the shoulders of special retainers when travelling beyond their territory. If the foot of a high *ali'i* touched the earth the very ground became sacred and taboo.

The principal gods of ancient Tahiti were the Polynesian deities, Ta'aroa, Tane, Tu and Ro'o. However, a shift in political power in the late seventeenth or early eighteenth century gave 'Oro, son of Ta'aroa, the place of supremacy in the Tahitian hierarchy of gods.

priests at Opoa in Ra'iatea were successful in elevating 'Oro and
o at the expense of Ta'aroa. This change of allegiance was
mpanied by considerable bloodshed until the 'Oro faction
ved all opposition. The symbol of 'Oro, god of war, was duly
lled at the Taputapuatea temple on Ra'iatea, and the 'Oro
extended to Mo'orea and Tahiti. The Arioi Society also
ted 'Oro and became its emissaries. When the Rev. John
ams travelled to Rarotonga from Ra'iatea in 1823, the first
ion he was asked was if 'Koro' (that is 'Oro) was still the
nant god in Tahiti.

e images of 'Oro (plate 43) are among the most remarkable
ucts of Tahitian art. They are stubby, cigar-shaped cylinders
sennit intricately plaited over a wood core. The eyes, nose,
h, arms, navel, and limbs were represented in varying degrees
npleteness. Attached to the images were tassels of red feathers,
h have now disappeared because of the ravages of insects
ime.

e cult of 'Oro reigned supreme until Pomare I decided to adopt Christianity in the second decade of the nineteenth century. His followers converted with him and the usual rampage of destruction of the temples and images soon followed. Almost everything reminiscent of pagan beliefs was destroyed and we are fortunate that about two dozen sennit images of 'Oro exist in museums today.

The symbols of Tahitian gods are termed *to'o*. Sometimes they are anthropomorphic, as is the case with 'Oro images, but the gods could also be represented by stones, by feathers, strings of sennit, pieces of shell, rainbows, birds, or almost any natural or artificial object.

The wooden anthropomorphic images, *ti'i*, served as vehicles of gods in the ancient Tahitian past, as indeed they did throughout most of eighteenth-century Polynesia. But when the cult of 'Oro gained power, or perhaps before that time, their use as images of gods was abandoned. It seems that sorcerers seized the opportunity to use *ti'i* in their profession, and so these wooden sculptures became the tools of black magicians. This Society Island move away from iconographic god symbols is related to a general trend of the more esoteric and priestly religions of Polynesia to adopt abstract symbols in preference to the more naturalistic sculptured forms.

Ti'i-type images were used for many purposes even after sorcerers took some up as convenient mediums. For example, they were used everywhere to mark the boundaries of territories, some being thirty feet in height with a totem-pole arrangement of figures standing one on top of the other. Canoe-stern pillars were often designed in this way (plates 2, 4, 37) when they were not merely

43. Sennit image of the war god 'Oro from the Society Islands. The cult of the Tahitian god 'Oro originated on the island of Ra'iatea, and then spread to Tahiti, where it supplanted Tangaroa as the supreme deity. Red feathers were the special symbol of 'Oro and were attached to the sennit body of god images such as this one. *Height: 19 in (47·5 cm). Cambridge, Museum of Archaeology and Ethnology*

44. A Tahitian carving with a pair of out-turned human images; another pair is repeated below in a highly conventionalized form. The use of this carving is unknown, but it is possibly from a canoe. *$6\frac{3}{4} \times 7\frac{1}{2}$ in (17·3 × 19 cm). London, British Museum*

individual figures fixed to the bow and stern (plate 36). The precise use of individual *ti'i* figures (plates 46-49) or the spirits they represent is not known. Some look like canoe carvings (plates 44, 49) while others (plates 16, 46, 47) have such a sinister expression that it is not difficult to visualize them as magician's dolls. Some *ti'i* were puppets used in story-telling and dramatic entertainment.

The stylistic character of Tahitian wooden images is known from a few examples. Some are unique, such as the double-headed *ti'i* (plate 47). The artistic style is variable but certain features are fairly consistent. For example, the head is domed and, by Polynesian iconographic standards, small in relation to the body. Emphasis is given to a protruding stomach, which is reasonable as the Tahitians believed the belly to be the centre of emotions and seat of the soul. The stance of *ti'i* is immobile, with no limb movement other than the occasional lifting of hand or hands to the chin. The sexual organs, if represented, are usually male and without emphasis. The feet are roughly blocked out, the legs and arms tend to be thin, while the hands typically rest on the abdomen. The face has a ridged jaw with eyes, ears, nose, and mouth well defined. The overall effect is one of dynamic vitality. These fragments of Tahitian sculptural art give us sufficient cause to lament the loss of figures, some of which must have exceeded in quality the best that have survived.

Funeral Rites

The most spectacular Tahitian artifact to survive is the mourner's costume (plates 50, 51). This ensemble consists of many parts: a shell mask with tropic-bird tail feathers, turban, shoulder cape, feather tassels, bark-cloth skirt with coconut discs attached, a wood crescent with pearl shells, and a curtain-like apron composed of minute pieces of mother-of-pearl shell linked together. The wearer also carried pearl-shell clappers and often a wooden club edged with shark teeth (plate 50). The effect of such costumes was both mysterious and frightening.

One of the most complete costumes (in the British Museum) (plate 51) is the more remarkable in that it was probably given by Captain Cook and resembles the one shown in the engraving in plate 50. Furthermore, when it was dismantled for cleaning in 1966, a Tahitian *ti'i* figure (plate 48) was found wrapped in bark-cloth to serve as a core for the head part. When this assemblage was put together is uncertain, but it could have been on HMS *Resolution*.

Such costumes were used in mourning rites intended to protect the spirit and body of the dead. The Society Islanders believed that from the moment of birth, human existence wavered between the two extremes of life *(ora)* and death *(pohe)*. In the event of a serious

45. A Tahitian godhouse carved in the form of a pig. Precious red feathers and the *to'o* symbols of the gods always received ritual care which included their storage in sacred containers when not in use. This is probably one such container. *Length: 34¼ in (87 cm). London, British Museum*

illness, the prospect of death was faced with equanimity, even if it was suspected that the illness was caused by sorcery. If death intervened, the kinsfolk of the dead lapsed into frantic mourning. All wailed loudly, lacerated their bodies with shells, stone flakes, and sharks' teeth until blood flowed freely. If the deceased was of high rank whole communities were transformed from happy-go-lucky villagers to distraught mourners who tore out hair, distorted their faces, and generally behaved like maniacs. When this first expression of grief subsided, speeches with poetic imagery eulogized the dead. Funeral rites proceeded with the corpse being either buried or placed in a ghost-house *(fare tupap'u)* (plate 50).

The corpse was semi-mummified by oiling, or was actually embalmed. Despite this, the hot humid air eventually decomposed the body, after which the bones were gathered, scraped, and then

46. *(Above left)* Wooden female image from the Society Islands. This small frowning figure with its right hand lifted to its mouth might have served either as a sorcerer's image or, more innocently, as a canoe carving. As is commonly the case with Tahitian images, no one knows exactly what this *ti'i* was used for. We do know that it was collected by the scientist Reinhold Foster who visited Tahiti in 1773 during Captain Cook's second Pacific expedition. *Height: $11\frac{3}{4}$ in (30 cm). Oxford, Pitt Rivers Museum*

47. *(Above)* Double-headed wooden figure from Tahiti. This unique Society Islands image, possibly used in sorcery, was acquired by the British Museum from Ireland, where it had reposed for over a century. The history of this superb work has been traced to a Captain Sampson Jervois R.N. of HMS *Dauntless*, a ship which visited Matavai Bay in 1822. *Height: 23 in (58·5 cm). London, British Museum*

48. *(Left)* A Tahitian image, found inside the head section of the Tahitian mourning dress in the British Museum, where it served as packing for the head for about two centuries (plate 51). It is possible that it was inserted into the costume aboard HMS *Resolution* and came to the British Museum in this condition. *Height: $18\frac{1}{3}$ in (46·5 cm). London, British Museum*

49. *(Right)* A *ti'i* image, probably from Tahiti. The Hunterian Museum records suggest that this figure was collected by Captain Cook at Aitutaki. However Captain Cook never went to Aitutaki but it is possible that the connection with Captain Cook is correct, and that the figure was collected in the Society Islands. The head with its angular jaw, the lips, nose, eyes and brows, resemble certain other images in the diverse Tahitian iconography. *Height: $15\frac{3}{4}$ in (40 cm). Glasgow, Hunterian Museum*

buried in the temple. The worst disaster that could befall a family was to have the bones of their dead relative stolen by enemies for conversion to fishhooks and chisels. Savage wars often followed such an event as outraged relatives sought quick revenge.

At the height of the mourning rites, priests patrolled in these costumes, accompanied by a near-naked band of soot-besmudged followers, all of whom were believed to be inspired by the spirit of the dead man. They set out in forays from the ghost-house, and were obliged to kill or injure anyone they met. Neighbouring inhabitants either fled to temples of refuge or hid in their houses. These strange rites continued until the participants changed their dress as an indication of their intention to desist, or until the local people started to attack the marauders.

50. This scene 'Drawn from Nature by W. Hodges' was engraved by W. Woollett and published in London in 1777. The caption on the engraving reads: 'A TOUPAPOW WITH A CORPSE ON IT– Attended by the chief Mourner in his Habit of Ceremony'. Grieving kinsfolk are to be seen below the platform bearing the shrouded body on the right, while on the left a costumed mourner appears with one of the many naked runners who usually accompanied the chief mourner.

51. Tahitian mourning dress, collected on Captain Cook's second Pacific voyage. When the dress was disassembled for cleaning in 1966, a wooden image was found inside the head section (plate 48).
120 in (303 cm). London, British Museum

The Austral Islands

52 and 53. An Austral Islands fly whisk, with a detail showing the figure at the end of the handle. The image is that of a Janus, with two out-turned figures joined at the back and sharing one torso. The heads have conventionalized faces, with a discernible mouth, nose and brows. The knobs on the top of the heads represent hair topknots rather than the ears or eyes they suggest to some observers. *Cambridge, Museum of Archaeology and Ethnology*

The Austral Islands are little known to the modern world even two centuries after their discovery by Western seafarers. Because contacts were brief and sporadic, very little was recorded of their ancient culture or the background to their traditional arts which, in many ways, are the finest of East Polynesia.

As far as the devastation of the native population is concerned, these islands rank as one of the saddest groups in the Pacific. Foreign diseases rapidly reduced the already small population to near extinction within decades after the first Western contacts. The advent of missionaries and foraging whalemen rapidly finished off a vigorous traditional culture that had sustained the people in health and good spirits for a thousand years. Here, as in many other parts of Polynesia, we must put most of the blame for the early destruction of traditional culture and its art on the well-meaning missionaries and their over-enthusiastic converts who were relentless in removing the evidence of their ancient religion.

Metal, of course, was unknown to the Austral Islanders, but as elsewhere, the first iron, obtained from passing ships, was quickly made into carving-tools. This stimulated the art of carving for a decade or so, followed by the usual degeneration and then extinction of traditional craft skills. Long after other forms of traditional decorative carving had ceased, however, a trade was carried on with ornately carved paddles. Curio-hungry sailors have always wanted something to take home to show where they had been, and to back up their stories of far, exotic places. Such Austral paddles, although good at their best, contrast unfavourably with the magnificent drums of Ra'ivavae, which were also sometimes made for trade.

The time scale of Austral art is of necessity brief for the simple reason that we know little about it before the advent of Europeans or indeed during the short period between their arrival and the time when the traditional craftsmen and their arts died out. Before beginning a more detailed discussion of Austral art, it is necessary to review briefly the physical environment of these islands, the nature of the aboriginal people, and the history of initial Western contacts. The Austral group, also known as the Tupua'i islands, forms an archipelago about four hundred miles south of Tahiti. A clear map or globe will show them running on a northwest-southeast axis, more or less in line with the Cook Islands, which form part of the same submarine mountain chain. The islands are, from west to east, Maria, Rimatara, Rurutu, Tupua'i, and Ra'ivavae. They stretch over a distance of five or six hundred miles.

Ra'ivavae and Tupua'i are of the high type of island with mountainous hinterlands, valleys, narrow coastal regions, and encircling coral reefs. Rurutu and Rimatara are of the *makatea* (upiifted-reef) type of island. The climate of the archipelago is colder than that of Tahiti, being further south. The islands are still tropical, but the cooler air and less fertile soil made for a more vigorous and rugged life, which was reflected in Austral manners.

The date of the first settlement is unknown. Vérin, in his work *L'Ancienne Civilisation de Rurutu* (Paris 1969), provides a radiocarbon figure of AD 1050 ±90, which accords with the general pattern of East Polynesian dispersal as anthropologists see it. The initial migration or migrations are believed to have originated from the Society Islands.

The first Western discovery of the Australs was made by Captain James Cook when HMS *Endeavour* came in from the north and ran up to the island of Rurutu on 14 August 1769. The Tahitian pilot, Tupaia, who had directed the course, immediately identified the island as 'Ohetiroa', that is, Hitiroa, the original name for Rurutu. It was Cook's intention to find out from the islanders if they knew of any lands to the south because a primary aim of this expedition was to look for the supposed continent of Terra Australis Incognita, which the European geographers insisted was somewhere in the South Pacific. A small continent was there, in the form of Antarctica, yet the happy people of the imagined land, who were said to use gold for the kitchen bowls and dance life away, were not to be seen. The reality for Cook on this day was a small isolated island, assailed by waves and peopled by natives who made no show of friendship.

The people of this southern archipelago proved to be more aggressive than the Tahitians, as the mutineers of HMS *Bounty* discovered in 1787 when they attempted to settle Tupua'i. The violence of the islanders persuaded the mutineers to leave, but not before some of their party were wounded and over sixty natives were killed. The London Missionary Society gained a foothold from about 1822, using native Tahitian converts. Epidemics, which swept hundreds to their deaths, were attributed to the anger of the Polynesian gods and for a time many turned back to the old religion. But such 'backsliding' was, it seems, mostly temporary.

The social organization of the Austral Islands appears to have followed the usual East Polynesian pattern of distinct class stratification. Chiefs inherited their authority over the commoners who were divided into several ranks. The extended family system of Polynesia prevailed, with public works done by communal labour. Because of the high island topography, villages were built on coastal lowlands adjacent to the fishing grounds of reef and open sea. The staple crops were *taro* (a root vegetable), coconut, and

54. Chief's seat, probably from the Austral Islands. Stools of this general form were often collected from Tahiti; but the small carvings set along the rim, which are similar to those on Austral fly whisks, suggest an Austral Island provenance. The height and length of chiefly seats were determined by the rank of the owner.
Cambridge, Massachusetts, Peabody Museum

sweet potato. Fish was commonly eaten, with the flesh of pig and fowl serving as an occasional luxury. Domestic equipment was much the same as in Tahiti, with bowls, *poi*-pounders, bark-cloth beaters, and anvils. War between tribal groups dominated life and gave rise to a fine range of weapons and chiefly regalia.

Sculptural art of the Austral Islands is known from a meagre scattering of mostly undocumented pieces. The two centres of carving were the island of Rurutu with its spectacular iconography and exquisite carved fly whisks, and the island of Ra'ivavae, which is well known for its 'ceremonial' paddles, ladles, and bowls. The Ra'ivavaean paddles are abundant in public and private collections. They teach us much about Austral surface decoration, yet their actual use remains uncertain because they are too frail to have been used as paddles. The ethnologist Martin Brunor believed that they were used on occasions of state, when one chief visited another. A further explanation, which does not preclude Brunor's, is that they were used as ceremonial dance paddles, which were used in Tonga and Easter Island.

56. *(Right)* **Group of fly whisk handles from the Austral and Society Islands. There has been some confusion about where individual fly whisks originally came from, for although the majority were collected in Tahiti, they were not necessarily made there.** *Collection James Hooper*

55. *(Above)* **Wood carving from Rurutu. This carving was collected on Captain Cook's first Pacific voyage which touched on Rurutu. Cook wrote of the occasion, 'that as one boat lay near the shore . . . some of them waded off to her and brought with them some trifles which they parted with for small nails'. The carving has two images on both sides, with dog figures as terminations, one of which is broken off. It may have been a canoe carving or a ridge piece to a small house.** *Length: 20½ in (52 cm). Cambridge, Museum of Archaeology and Ethnology*

The excellence of Austral Island bark-cloth is known from museum specimens. As in many parts of Polynesia, this was the last craft to survive because it had many uses after woven cloth had supplanted it as a dress material. Traditionally bark-cloth was used for clothing, bed covers, wrappings for precious objects, and as winding sheets for the dead. Brunor interviewed old women of the Australs who remembered the communal bark-cloth work parties of their childhood, when as many as twenty women would sit beating away. From a distance the sound of this activity was like the roll of far-off thunder.

Carving

The iconography of the Australs is little known, nor are its meanings understood. The few wooden images that survived destruction by converts to Christianity suggest a once rich range of image types. The most wonderful Austral image that has come to us

57 and 58. *(Overleaf)* **Front and back views of the god A'a from Rurutu. This image is one of the truly great works of Polynesian wood sculpture. The cavity at the back, which has its own cover not shown here, contained separate small images.** *Height: 44 in (112 cm). London, British Museum*

from the early nineteenth century is a Rurutuan figure of the god A'a (plates 57, 58). This was taken to Ra'iatea in 1821 to join the collection of missionary trophies. It is male and has small 'human' forms sprouting out from head and body, a feature which helped perpetuate a long-held misidentification of this carving as the Polynesian creator-god Tangaroa giving birth to mankind. A cavity in the back housed a number of small images which have since been lost. The stance of the body, the thin arms, the placement of hands on belly, and the domed head with sharp jaw ridge of this image relate it to the Tahitian type of wooden *ti'i*.

A departure from East Polynesian wood-carving conventions as we see them is found in the curious Rurutuan carving which has two-sided figures and a dog in its composition (plate 55). It has no known use but it may have come from a canoe or served as a ridge piece. The nearest sculptural resemblance to it is a rare New Zealand Maori carving, commonly called the 'Kaitaia lintel', in the Auckland Museum.

A wide variety of anthropomorphic images of the Janus type (with double and outfacing figures joined at the back) is seen at the lower end of Rurutuan fly whisk handles (plates 52, 56). The earliest records show some of these to be from Rurutu; their prevalence in Tahiti, however, and the eighteenth-century use of the label 'Otaheiti' for almost anything from East Polynesia obscured for a century or so their Austral Island origin. Some fly whisk handles, such as those with a single image on the right and the left of the central specimens (plate 56), are Society Island in style, as is the distinctive type of handle made in sections from sperm whale ivory (plate 62).

Austral stone images are likewise little known, yet they are often very fine. They are sometimes highly finished, such as the female deity from Ra'ivavae, in the Pitt Rivers Museum. A large female image carried to Tahiti from Ra'ivavae is now to be seen outside the Musée Gauguin, Tahiti (plate 63), where it imparts some of the grandeur of the Polynesian past.

The genius of the Ra'ivavaean wood-carver is evident from the many small carvings that have survived. The carving in plate 55 has dancing figures on it which are very similar to those on paddles (plates 64, 66) and drums (plates 68, 69). These rows of dancing figures, so prevalent in Ra'ivavaean wood carving, are often so conventionalized that they form abstract patterns. The evolution of this abstraction is indicated by a rubbing from a drum cleat (plate 61) showing the merging of figures. Such intricacy of carved surface decoration is seen elsewhere in Polynesia, notably on Tongan clubs and Mangaian ceremonial adzes.

59 and 60. Female figure from Ra'ivavae. Only a few examples of freestanding figures from the Austral Islands have survived. This one was acquired by the British Museum in 1854 from Sir George Grey who was Governor General of New Zealand. The carving style relates it to images seen on the base sections of drums. The 'sun' motifs are placed on cheeks, breasts, and knees. *Height: 24⅜ in (62 cm). London, British Museum*

61. *(Left)* Stone image from Ra'ivavae in the Austral Islands. Rendered in well-dressed stone, this figure follows the conventions of Ra'ivavaean woodcarving. The sex is female, as is usual in the carved figures of this island. *Height: 37⅜ in (95 cm). Oxford, Pitt Rivers Museum*

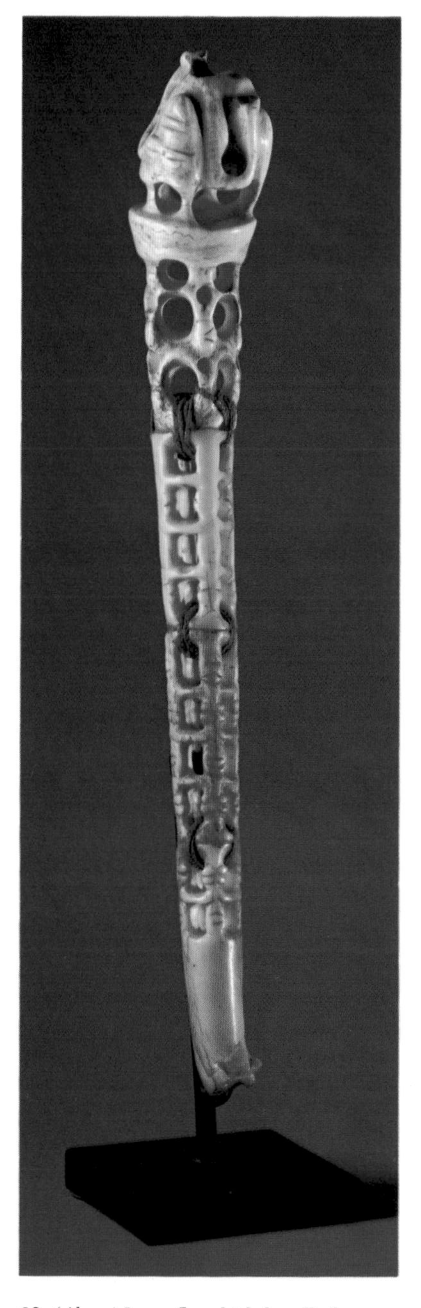

62. *(Above)* Ivory fly-whisk handle from Tahiti. The source of ivory was the teeth of stranded sperm whales although later on, whalemen brought in walrus ivory. The short lengths have been joined with sennit. *Height: 11¾ in (30 cm). New York, Metropolitan Museum*

63. A massive stone figure from Ra'ivavae, which was carried to Tahiti by ship in 1933 along with another figure of almost equal size. Heavy stone sculpture was made in the Marquesas Islands, from where the East Polynesian tradition derives. *Height: 107½ in (272 cm). Tahiti, Musée Gauguin*

64. *(Left)* Enlarged detail of a paddle illustrated in plate 67, from Ra'ivavae. This enlargement provides a close-up view of the 'sun', human image and crescent motifs. Ra'ivavaean decoration relies on the repetitive use of a few motifs with ingenious adaptation of them to paddles, drums, ladles, bowls, and other objects. *Height of blade: 8 in (23 cm). Cambridge, Museum of Archaeology and Ethnology*

65. *(Above)* Rubbing from a drum cleat from Ra'ivavae showing linked figures with heads at both top and bottom, which helps illustrate the evolution of surface patterns of the Ra'ivavaean carver. If the heads are removed, the rows of the human figure motif create the common zigzag pattern. *Width of cleat: $2\frac{1}{4}$ in (7 cm). From a drum in the Hancock Museum*

66. *(Right)* Head of a decorative paddle illustrated in plate 67, from Ra'ivavae. This enlargement shows that nineteenth-century Ra'ivavaean carving survived as a high-level Polynesian art form, at least in some of its smaller works. *Cambridge, Museum of Archaeology and Ethnology*

The great stimulus to latter day Ra'ivavaean carving was the value of such objects as trade items. In a land almost bereft of saleable man-made products, these carvings were traded through the early decades of the nineteenth century for goods from passing whalers and other ships that called for water, hogs, root crops, and such relaxation and refreshment as the island could provide.

An unusual artifact, probably created by this carving trade, is a form of ladle (plate 73). It is evidently derived from the traditional bowls (plate 70) but has a paddle-type handle added to it to form an unusual hybrid. There is no suggestion that the two parts were ever joined as a European craftsman might join two parts of a

67. *(Above)* Paddles of various shapes from Ra'ivavae. The paddle standing on the right is an example of the oldest type, being small and delicate in form. The taller centre paddle is of relatively early date but has some of the latter-day massiveness. The two lying flat have squared handles, a common feature of post-contact paddles, while the one standing on the left is a hybrid between the two forms, with a round handle and a squared top. A detail from the diamond bladed paddle is shown in enlargement in plate 64. *Cambridge, Museum of Archaeology and Ethnology*

68 and 69. *(Right and left)* Ceremonial drum from Ra'ivavae with detail showing cleat section. Heavy sennit cords were used to pull the sharkskin tympanum, the pull being taken up by cleats which usually had carved ends (left, plate 68). The carved base of the drum has seven rows of dancing female figures, with multiple crescents set in vertical groups below each row. *Height: 50 in (127 cm). Cambridge, Museum of Archaeology and Ethnology*

70. *(Above left)* Wooden bowl from Ra'ivavae. Small figures, similar to those found on the tops of certain paddles, are here seen at one end of this bowl. The undersurface is entirely carved with the geometrical design of the 'headless' human figures. *25½ × 12 in (64·7 × 30·5 cm). Christchurch, Canterbury Museum*

71. *(Left)* Whalebone bowl from Rurutu. This fine oval bowl, with a pouring lip, has nine relief figures on each side and two 'pig' figures at one end. *14½ × 6½ in (37 × 16·3 cm). Auckland, Auckland Museum*

72 and 73. *(Right and above)* Ra'ivavaean ladles, with detail. The smallest here seems to be the oldest and most utilitarian in form. The one on the left, also of fine quality, has retained the round handle, and has two decorative birds which are reproduced in detail in plate 72. *Cambridge, Museum of Archaeology and Ethnology*

74. A group of breast ornaments from Rurutu. The pearl-shell necklace at the top measuring 55 in (139·7 cm) was collected in about 1823 by the missionary G. Bennet of the London Missionary Society and was worn by 'female chiefs'. The three lower necklaces, averaging 16½ in (42 cm) in length, consist of a base cord of twisted coir with braided human hair bound round. The attached miniature carvings in ivory represent human testicles, pigs, and chiefs' seats. The 'reel' symbols have no known meaning. *Collection James Hooper*

chair. Polynesians preferred to work from a solid block of wood, even when working with such large objects as the seat shown in plate 54.

The Rurutuan ability to shape bone ivory and shell is clearly seen in the bowl made from the jawbone of a whale (plate 71), and the 'phallic' necklaces and shell breast ornament (plate 74). Scholars have argued about the meaning of the small necklace attachments as well as the identity of the little animal (plate 75). There seems to be little doubt that the double balls represent human testicles, while the small creature is evidently a pig rendered to suggest a phallus in the Polynesian 'double-theme' manner of carving; the flared oblong ornaments appear to represent the seats of chiefly authority.

75. A 'pig' unit from a Rurutuan necklace. Although necklace units such as this one are sometimes thought to represent dogs, they look more like pigs; and this identification is supported by the fact that pigs symbolized power and wealth in ancient East Polynesia. *1¼ in (3 cm). Cambridge, Museum of Archaeology and Ethnology*

The Cook Islands

The Cook Islands are divided physically and culturally into two widely scattered groups designated today as the Northern and Southern Cook Islands (see map p. 9). The northern group are nearer to Samoa than they are to Rarotonga, the largest island in the Southern Cook Islands; the ethnographic relationship in ancient times between the two groups was not sufficient to link them together as a unit, and their modern association is chiefly for administrative reasons.

The northern isles are coral atolls on which life was a struggle for survival: while they developed a remarkable material culture suitable for atoll-living, making fine matting, tools, canoes and domestic utensils, their only decorative art now known to us was a specialized craft of using pearl-shell inlay on canoes and paddles. Their culture, therefore, lies largely outside the scope of this book.

The Southern Cook Islands are a traditionally related group which vary from atolls, in the case of Takutea and Manuae, to the high volcanic island of Rarotonga which rises 2,100 feet above the sea. The other islands are of the *makatea* type, formed by submarine upheavals of ancient coral atolls and reefs. Inter-tribal wars were frequent on individual islands, and occasionally between islands. Political activity tended to centre on particular islands; Rarotonga has always played an important role, as it does today. The chiefs of Atiu gained ascendancy over Mauke and Mitiaro. A remarkable and more-or-less homogeneous style of carving evolved which had special developments in each island—Rarotonga is notable for its fisherman's gods and staff-gods, Mangaia for its ceremonial adzes, Atiu for its wooden seats, and Mitiaro, Atiu and Mauke for their wonderful mace and slab gods.

From the evidence available it appears that the southern Cook group was settled by Polynesian sea rovers over a period commencing about 800 AD. Legends refer to the homeland of 'Avaiki, which is almost certainly Ra'iatea in the Society Islands (which was originally called Havai'i). Rarotonga claims a Samoan sea king among its earliest settlers, yet it is clear that the basic culture originated from the Society Islands.

The discovery of the Cook Islands by Westerners has as varied a history as the islands themselves. The Spanish explorer, Mendaña, is said to have seen Pukapuka when he passed it in 1595. Shortly afterwards, in 1606, his countryman, Quiros, is said to have discovered Rakahanga. The first positive Western discovery of the Southern Cook Islands was made by Captain Cook in 1773 who found Manuae, and named it Hervey Island—a name which was synonymous with the Cook Islands well into the present century (the term is found in museum registers, especially in England). In

76. Fisherman's canoe god from Rarotonga. The formal Cook Island *ti'i* features are particularly strong in this example of a fisherman's talisman. The inturning of the feet is said to adapt these images to a canoe prow. Painted tattoo patterns appear on the front, back, and sides of this figure. *Height: 16¾ in (42·5 cm). Cambridge, Massachusetts, Peabody Museum*

1777 Cook discovered Mangaia, Atiu, and Takutea, but as these islands lacked sheltered harbours they escaped the attention of other early seafarers. Rarotonga's risky anchorages made it a dangerous port of call for nineteenth-century sailing ships while the expansive lagoon at Aitutaki was inaccessible to ships. As for the other Cook Islands, waves pounded on their ledge-like reefs and against their eroded cliffs, making them so uninviting that the inhabitants were spared the usual flood of whalers and traders. Such hazards did not, however, deter missionaries.

A station of the London Missionary Society was set up on Aitutaki in 1821 and it was from there that the Rev. John Williams and his party foraged out to Rarotonga, Mauke, and Mitiaro seeking souls with as much enthusiasm as they attacked all that appeared to them to represent 'heathenism'. Their Christian converts joined in the destruction of 'idols' with the usual Polynesian zest. Imported diseases swept through the population and reduced it to a mere remnant of what it was, and so the familiar pattern of the demise of a traditional Polynesian culture, along with its sculptural and ritual arts, was reenacted in these islands.

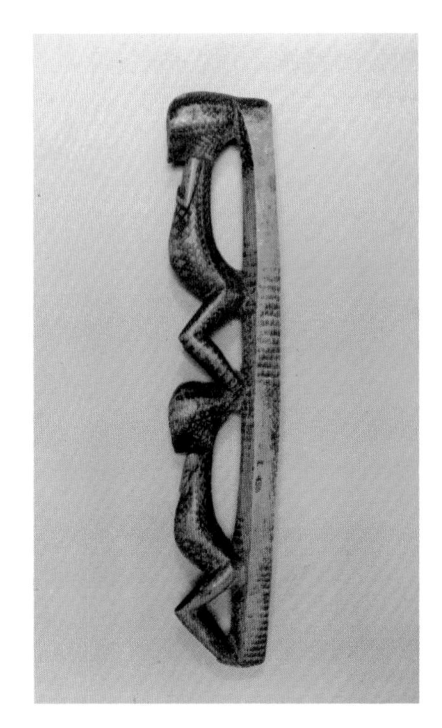

77. *(Above)* **Post with two carved and painted figures from the Cook Islands. The side view of this carving illustrates the repetitive rhythms often seen in Cook Islands and Austral Islands art.** *Height: 15⅜ in (39 cm). Glasgow, Hunterian Museum*

78. *(Above right)* **A hand club from Rarotonga. The edges are notched to make serrations, and an out-turned figure adorns the pommel. The holes in the blade would have been used to attach feather bundles and those at the butt end might have taken a wrist thong, both features occurring in New Zealand clubs.** *Length: 12¼ in (31 cm). Cambridge, Museum of Archaeology and Ethnology*

79. *(Right)* **Serrated pole clubs from Rarotonga. As a rule, the blade parts measure somewhat more than one-third of the total length. The eyes set below the blades, and the teeth serrations, give credence to the theory that this design has an animalistic origin, and perhaps derives from the crocodile motifs of Indonesia and Melanesia.** *Length (left to right): 103½ in (263 cm); 100 in (254 cm); 102 in (259 cm) and 106½ in (270·5 cm). Collection James Hooper*

Houses

The villages of the Cook Islands were picturesque, with dwellings widely dispersed. The ground plan of houses was basically quadrangular. Although the climate was tropical, the winters were sufficiently cold to necessitate walled houses. The structure consisted of posts to which beams were lashed to form a frame, with thatch placed on the roof. Buildings varied as much in type and function as did the quality of their workmanship; they ranged from domestic huts, cooking sheds, and sleeping houses, to canoe houses and large houses of entertainment.

Small godhouses, termed *are ei 'au* or 'houses for peace', were among the sacred structures. In times of war the islanders sometimes abandoned their villages to take refuge elsewhere, but their first obligation on their return was to restore their godhouses if they had become damaged or dilapidated. Such godhouses were kept empty as it was firmly believed that the spirit of the god took up residence within them. Other special houses were set aside for slit gongs, drums, and special possessions. Consecrated houses called *'are vananga* served as places of sacred learning. Sacred structures were especially well made with their parts held together by decorative sennit lashing of a high order.

Decorative house carvings formerly existed, yet it seems not in any great abundance. The Rev. W. W. Gill mentions the carved thresholds of Mangaia houses, while the Rev. John Williams,

writing in his book *Missionary Enterprises*, describes a chapel built by the well-meaning Rarotongans for the use of missionaries that was decorated in a manner contrary to puritanical taste. He says of this house:

'One of its most striking pecularities was the presence of many indelicate heathen figures carved on the centre posts. This was accounted for from the circumstance, that, when built, a considerable part of the people were heathens; and, as a portion of the work was allotted to each district, unaccompanied by specific directions as to the precise manner of its performance, the builders thought that the figures with which they decorated the maraes would be equally ornamental in the main pillars of a Christian sanctuary. The building was 250 feet in length, and 40 feet wide.'

The 'objectionable' carvings were in all probability nothing more offensive than figures with visible sexual organs, such as one finds in the house carvings of New Zealand and the Marquesas Islands, innocent enough yet shocking to nineteenth-century missionary sensibility.

The particular glory of house building centred on the magnificent sennit lashings similar in character to those of Samoa and Tonga. An impression of the skill involved can be got by looking at the lashings of Mangaian adzes (plates 101-103). Certain church buildings, which were constructed in the nineteenth century and survived into the twentieth century, show beautiful plait work of this kind. Plaiting with fine sennit is a distinctive and diverse Polynesian art. Before the coming of metal nails it was essential to both canoe and house building. The woven baskets, platters, mats, and fans of the Cook Islands reached a high point of craft artistry; fans were either quickly made from a coconut leaflet or laboriously plaited from dressed materials of a narrow weft about a quarter inch in width. The superior fans were plaited on a wooden handle with a narrow tang which supported the triangular blade. The finer Rarotongan fans (plate 81) were frequently carved at the butt end of the handle with anthropomorphic 'Janus' figures, while the grip part of the handle was decorated with plaited sennit, sometimes in combination with a fine plait of human hair. Fans often symbolized chiefly rank and, in their own right, are a distinctive Polynesian art form. The Cook Island fans compare favourably with the best fans of the Hawaiian and Marquesan islands.

The highest arts of the Cook Islands were the religious arts supported by the high chiefs *(ariki)* and the lesser chiefs *(rangatira)*. Genealogical standing determined the position of the individual in the social hierarchy. A tribal style of life prevailed with land divided

80. *(Above left)* **The extraordinarily fine quality of Cook Island sennit plaiting is evident from this illustration which shows three belts, a fan and a basket.** *Lengths: fan: 32½ in (82·5 cm); belts: approx. 216 in (550 cm); basket: 26½ in (67·3 cm). Collection James Hooper*

81. *(Above)* **A group of three fans from Rarotonga. The wooden part is usually decorated at the butt end while the grip has ornate binding. The slender upper part of the handle serves as a tang to which the body of the fan is woven. The carved ends are often marvellous abstractions of the human form, typically with the heads and bodies facing outwards in the manner of a Janus.** *Length: approximately 19 in. Cambridge, Museum of Archaeology and Ethnology*

82. A striking chief's headdress of the Aitutakian type, formed of a sennit-bound frame and cap, with human hair and feathers attached. It is thought that this type of headdress, seen in the print of Te Pou (plate 1), was peculiar to Aitutaki. *39¾ × 12¼ in (101 × 31 cm). Cambridge, Museum of Archaeology and Ethnology*

amongst the chiefs in order of rank, who in turn parcelled out plots to their followers. Priestly experts *(ta'unga)* included specialists skilled in religious ritual, chanting, carving, and any other occupations that called for long training and professional devotion. Rules relating to sanctity, developed from concepts of *mana* and *tapu*, controlled both secular and sacred life, but with less severity than in Tahiti. The great gods of the Polynesian pantheon–Tangaroa, Tane, Tu and Rongo–were all given their due worship with regional modifications of religious ritual.

Warfare was extensively practised and inspired an art of its own. The ironwood pole clubs of Rarotonga are superb in the precision

83. Fisherman's god from Rarotonga. This weathered god shows better than most the thick-set, short, sturdy body and well-formed head typical of this kind of image. The carving is bold and direct. It also illustrates the prudery of foreign collectors who amputated the sexual organs of carvings. *Height: $17\frac{1}{2}$ in (44 cm). London, British Museum*

84 and 85. Two views of a fisherman's god from Rarotonga. The extensive tattoo patterns are a distinctive feature of this impressive god. The side view shows that the head and body are of nearly identical size and that the head is carved in a similar style to the staff gods. The feet have typical notching on the underside. The enlargement of the ears, also notched, and of the umbilicus, are common features of Rarotongan images. *Height: 12¾ in (31·5 cm). London, British Museum*

of their craftsmanship (plate 79); the labour of cutting such graceful and balanced weapons from a block of wood, which needed to be at least as wide as the widest part of the blade, is a marvel of patient craftsmanship.

Clothes

Head ornaments were the delight of the Cook Islanders as they were of the Tahitians. They vary from flower and leaf wreaths worn for a day and then cast aside, to the elaborate feathered helmets of the chiefs. Feather headbands, turbans of bark-cloth, and cone-shaped sennit caps were also commonly worn. Eye shades protected the eyes of fishermen working on dazzling seas, while

cone-shaped coir caps, a speciality of the island of Atiu, served to protect the heads of warriors. The high feather headdresses of these islands are obviously related to the Tahitian forms which have already been mentioned, but those of the Rarotongan and Aitutakian chiefs stand in a special class of their own. They are superb examples of the use of feathers which conceal a complexity of craft-work including a sennit-lashed base-frame and a coir cap. The long, thin feathers used came from the tails of tropic birds and were highly prized. Only a few feathers could be obtained from each bird and it was sometimes necessary to voyage considerable distances to obtain a good supply—the atoll of Manuae was regarded as a fruitful source of such feathers.

The portrait of the Rarotongan chief, Te Po, or Te Pou (plate 1), conveys some of the glory of the Cook Island *ali'i* wearing a high headdress. He also carries a triangular fan and a spear which combined with his bodily tattoo give a striking effect, to say the

86 and 87. Wooden image from Rarotonga with a detail showing the supplementary figures on the chest. This striking figure is closely related to the Ortiz figure (plate 88); both are lucky in having escaped emasculation. The style of both heads, with their high domed foreheads, large elliptical mouths, eyes and brows, is distinctively Rarotongan and is reminiscent of fisherman's gods. It is not known what god or ancestor they represented. *Height: 27⅛ in (69 cm). London, British Museum*

88. Wooden image with supplementary figures from Rarotonga. A singularly dynamic piece of Polynesian sculpture, this work was brought to England by Mr Armitage, a member of the London Missionary Society who worked on Tahiti, Rarotonga and Mo'orea as an artisan employed to teach Polynesians the art of cotton spinning. The identity of the carving is unknown. The powerful head, round belly, and vigorous male stance are expressive. The zigzag carving on the feet to represent toes is a notable feature. *Height: 22¼ in (56·5 cm). Collection George Ortiz*

89. *(Overleaf)* Wooden image, probably from the island of Aitutaki. The base which supports this figure has been cut from a larger object, probably a canoe. Carvings in human form are rarely seen from Aitutaki, possibly because there was a preference there for the slab-type ritual carvings. The head style resembles that of Rarotongan carvings while the arms and legs have an elongation to a 'matchstick' form. The back is straight, with belly and buttocks protruding in an almost comical manner. A low-relief serrated edge and a raised zigzag bar cross the chest horizontally. *Height: 16 in (40·6 cm). Glasgow, Hunterian Museum*

least. Unfortunately, little is known of Cook Island tattoo designs.

Cook Island clothing basically consisted of a loin cloth *(maro)* for men and the short skirt wrap-around *(pareu)* for women, but ponchos *(tiputa)*, rectangular capes and plaited girdles were also worn. War chiefs had coir helmets, and plaited waist bands which probably served to hold small weapons in the New Zealand Maori manner.

The decorative ritual carvings may be divided into five major categories:

(a) fisherman's gods and other anthropomorphic wooden images from Rarotonga;
(b) god images with secondary figures from Rarotonga;
(c) staff gods with anthropomorphic heads and phallic ends;
(d) mace and slab gods from the Atiu-Mitaro-Mauke cluster of islands;
(e) ceremonial adzes from Mangaia.

We shall consider each of these categories in turn.

Fisherman's gods (plates 76, 83-85): These were carved on the island of Rarotonga from dense hardwood blocks. They are characteristically free-standing, short and thick-set in stature with heads almost as large as the body. They have a protruding belly with a pronounced navel sometimes shaped in a ring. The buttocks are enlarged, which strengthens a stolid yet dynamic stance. The male sex is indicated by a large penis that reaches almost to the feet. Seen in profile (plate 85), such images show a rhythm in the arrangement of parts which is at first surprising as these images are essentially bulky. The line of the chest and stomach swings outward, then is reversed by an equally vital line which moves from the buttock to the knee, switches in direction at the ankle, then moves forward along the foot. The feet are inturned, presumably to help fit any image into the bows of a canoe. The massive domed head has large ears, large crescent eyes and brows, and an equally large mouth. These features combine to create a strong impression. Tattoo patterns are painted on a few of the extant images (e.g. plates 76, 84).

God images with secondary figures (plates 86-88): The two representatives of this class of image shown here seem to be the only survivors of what was probably a relatively abundant type. Both are of Rarotongan origin and were probably collected by early missionaries. They possess the main characteristics of the fisherman's gods about the head and body but they are much more drawn out vertically. Also, they have the supplementary figures

90. **Staff god from Rarotonga. The inner rolls of bark-cloth are white and brown, with an outer layer of cloth ornamented with a zigzag pattern. The sennit bindings and the generally undamaged state of this staff god make it unusual.** *Length: 45 in (114 cm). Dunedin, Otago Museum (W. O. Oldman Collection)*

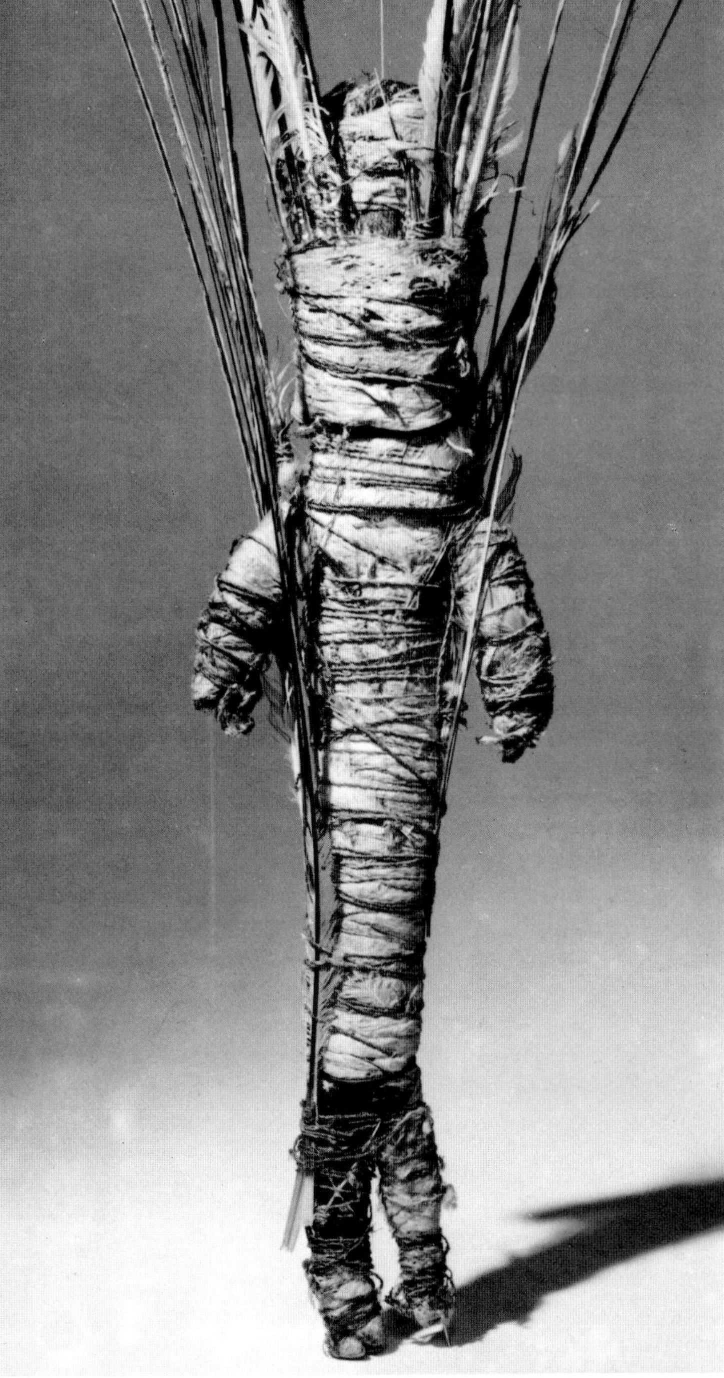

91. **This image from Mangaia is made of folded lengths of sennit, wrapped up in white bark-cloth. Feathers, including the red tail feathers of the tropic bird, were attached to it, but have now largely disintegrated. The actual shape of the image may have been less important than the materials used to create it: feathers were sacred and, on Mangaia, sennit represented the god of fertility, Tane. This work was collected by the Rev. John Williams who said it was regarded as embodying the progenitor of the inhabitants of Mangaia.** *Length: $17\frac{1}{4}$ in (44 cm). Cambridge, Museum of Archaeology and Ethnology*

which resemble the bat-like secondary figures of staff gods. The surfaces of this type are smoothed and polished.

Aitutaki produced images of a type intermediate in style between Rarotongan figures and the Tahitian *ti'i* (plate 89). The few Aitutakian images extant have elongated bodies with a back that runs straight down from squared and sharply ridged shoulders. Skinny legs and equally skinny arms, with hands resting on a protruberant belly, seem to be characteristic but little is known of the iconography of Aitutaki.

93 and 94. *(Above and right)* **A staff god from Rarotonga, showing the staff and bark-cloth bundle.** *London, British Museum*

92. *(Left)* **Upper portion of a staff god from Rarotonga. This side view illustrates well the alternation of the bat-like secondary figures. Because it was inconvenient to carry the larger gods back whole to England in the cramped quarters of sailing ships, it was a common practice to cut the top part off.** *Height: 25⅜ in (64·5 cm). Cambridge, Massachusetts, Peabody Museum*

Staff god images (plates 90, 92-95): In this category of Rarotongan carvings we see the same artistic conventions used in the fisherman's gods and those images with secondary figures described above. The staff gods, which were between about 30 inches (76 mm) and eighteen feet (6 m) in length, were carved from ironwood. The surfaces were either burnished smooth or left relatively rough and unpolished. The upper end is surmounted by

95. *(Left)* Upper portion of a staff god from Rarotonga. This fragment is from the upper end of a large staff god, probably about twelve feet long if the relative proportions of complete staff gods are used as a measure. This three-quarter view of the upper portion reveals the flattened form of the heads of such images. The features are the same as those seen in the truly three-dimensional fisherman's gods of Rarotonga. The illustration also shows how the secondary figures below the head of the god are single when in the profile position, and double when facing outwards. The austere, aloof dignity of the principal heads of these carvings is admirably seen in this one. *Height: 28½ in (72·5 cm). Cambridge, Museum of Archaeology and Ethnology*

96 and 97. *(Right)* Two mace gods from the Cook Islands, which are of a relatively simple design. They have a vertical succession of loops which are largely derived from the human form. The resemblance of these loops to the relatively naturalistic Cook Island carving now in the Hunterian Museum (plate 77) enables us to speculate as to what they represent. The handles of these maces are bound with sennit cords, some of which were designed to hold tufts of feathers. *Length: left: 33½ in (85 cm); right: 55 in (140 cm). London, British Museum.*

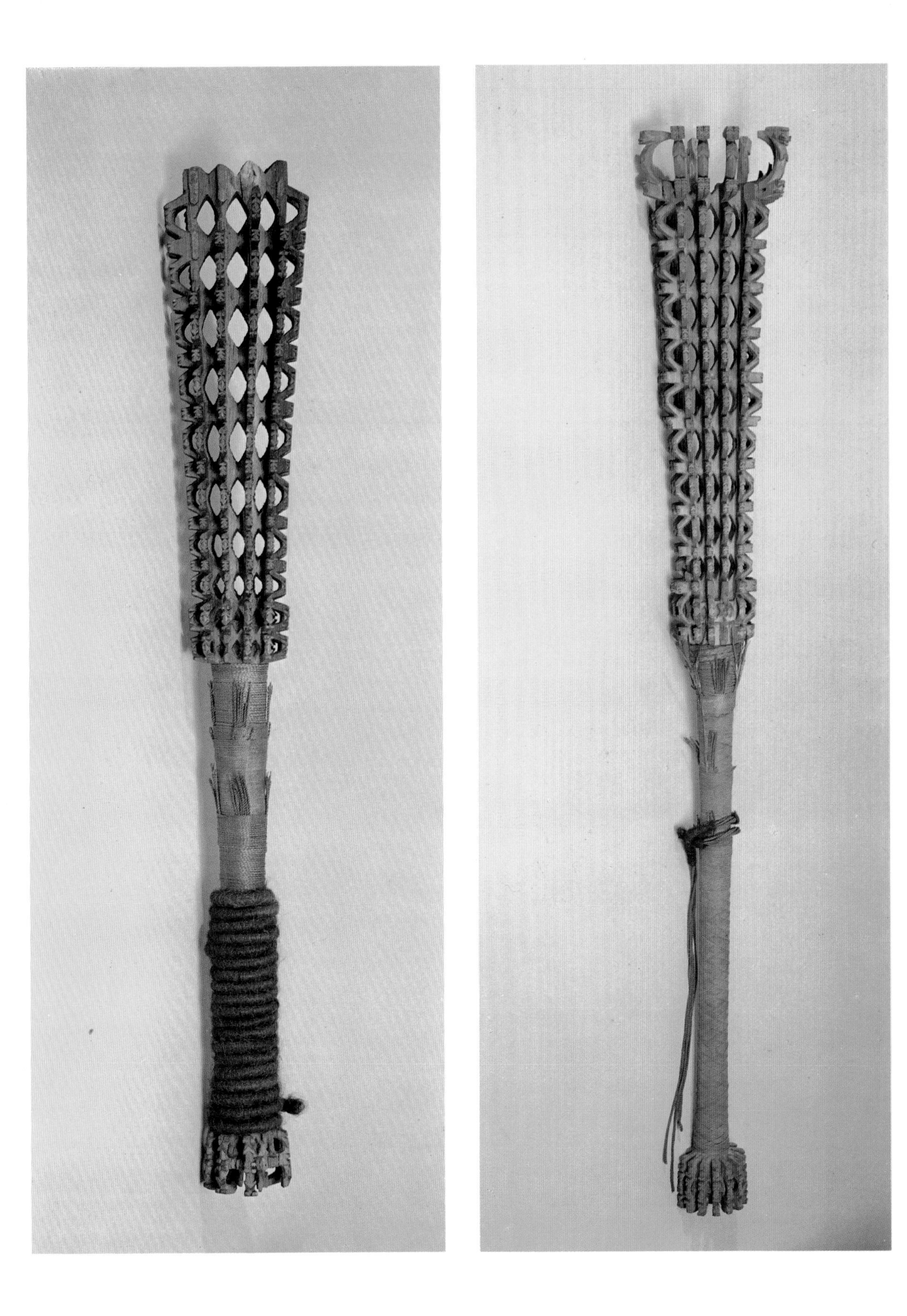

a flattened head with 'arms' immediately below it, while the lower end terminates in a phallus. Just below the head, and above the phallic end, are placed bat-like figures rendered alternately full-face and in profile. The central part or 'body' of the staff god has a large roll of bark-cloth (plate 90) or, when the bark-cloth is missing, a blank shaft. According to missionary accounts pieces of polished pearl shell and red feathers were placed within the bark-cloth roll near the interior shaft to represent the soul of the god. Rarotongan staff gods have suffered such vandalism at the hands of Europeans that only a few have the bark-cloth rolls intact. Frequently only the head part has been retained as it was the custom for staffs to be cut up for transport back to England. The phallic ends were removed because such sexual features were considered obscene and certainly not suitable to be viewed by Victorian ladies. The role of sexual organs in Polynesian art as symbols of chiefly vitality and the continuity of tribal life was quite beyond the narrow-minded missionaries.

Mace and slab gods (plates 96-100): These curious images, sometimes referred to as 'district gods', are among the most precious objects of East Polynesian art. Almost all that are extant were collected by early missionaries, mainly those associated with the London Missionary Society. They vary in form from the relatively simply carved 'slabs' to the mace gods which have ornate decoration and resemble the ritual maces of Europe. The mace gods have elaborate heads set above a long handle which has in turn a similarly decorated pommel. Sennit binding was used on handles, with attached bundles of feathers, but only remnants of the latter have survived. Sennit and feathers were thought to attract and accommodate the gods, and thus were regarded as more important than the wooden part which we today treasure as sculpture.

The process of carving mace gods is an intricate study which has been analysed by Buck in his *Arts and Crafts of the Cook Islands* (Honolulu 1944). He describes how they were carved from a wooden block, and squared to a rectangular cross section. This was cut into, leaving vertical channels and outstanding pillars. The pillars were carved to designs that resulted in pierced work with complex looped figures, chevrons, and other secondary motifs. The anthropomorphic origin of the loops is well conveyed by comparing them with more naturalist renderings of this type, notably that of the Cook Island carving in plate 77.

Slab gods from the island of Aitutaki are normally simple and flat. They are 18 inches or more high, with blades that taper from a broad top to a narrow-handled base. The frontal surfaces

98 and 99. Upper part of a mace god from Mauke, with detail. The loop carvings and lugs, which appear to be anthropomorphic, are clearly seen in this illustration. *Height: 9¼ in (23·5 cm). Cambridge, Museum of Archaeology and Ethnology*

100. A magnificent mace god from Mangaia, which is described by Oldman in his catalogue as 'One of the great tribal deities of Mangaia'. The flared head was carved by cutting channels or 'pillars' in a shaped block of wood, then working out the various abstracted anthropomorphic elements, raised lozenges, chevron flanges and transverse bands. No single carvings in Polynesia exceed these mace gods in sheer complexity except New Zealand canoes and house carvings. *Height: 43 in (109 cm). Dunedin, Otago Museum*

101. Group of three nineteenth-century trade adzes from Mangaia. These three adzes all possess the true ceremonial flat blades, a feature which usually suggests early post-contact manufacture as the old blades were soon used up in manufacture of adzes for trade. The Mangaian trade-adze makers were obliged to turn to working adze blades as substitutes which were readily obtained as they were cast aside in favour of metal. The pedestal adze on the left is so beautiful in all its features that one is tempted to believe pedestal ceremonial adzes existed in ancient times. The standing adze on the right is of good quality, while that lying flat is an example of the exaggeration of the original forms which was to lead to the grotesque before this remarkable craft was extinguished. *Cambridge, Museum of Archaeology and Ethnology*

102. A detail of the pedestal adze on the left of plate 101, showing the superb lashing.

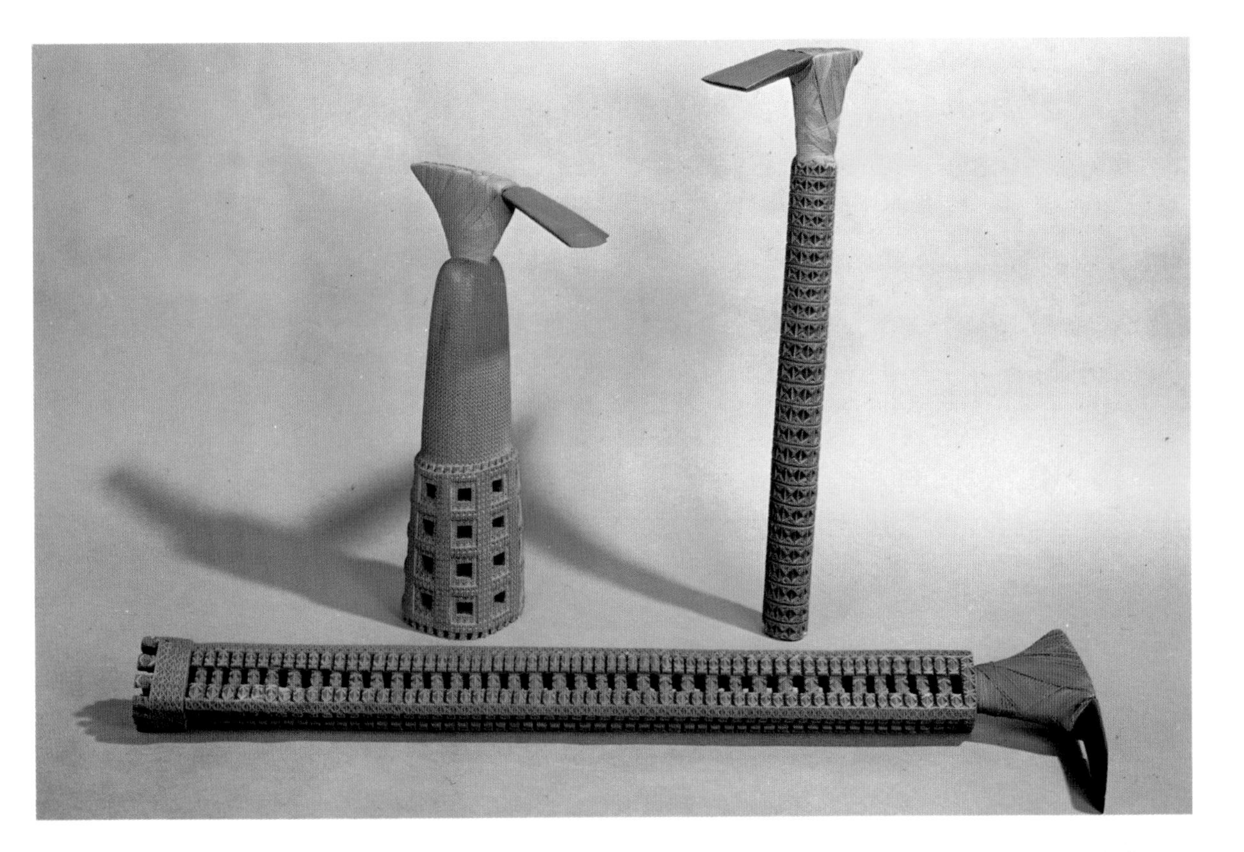

are quite elaborately decorated with raised or sunken chevrons, triangles, lozenges, and other motifs. Associated with these slab gods are certain carvings from Aitutaki which have a human head or whole images at the top of a decorated slab or post-like base.

Ceremonial adzes (plates 101-103): These adzes were made in Mangaia, and probably represented gods or spirits. They are known as ceremonial adzes because of an important passage in the Rev. W. W. Gill's book, *Jottings from the Pacific* (London 1885):

'The stone adzes were secured to their wooden hafts by means of fine sinnet, itself esteemed divine. It was fabled that the peculiar way in which the natives of Mangaia fasten their axes was originally taught them by the gods. A famous god, named Tanemataariki, i.e., Tane-of-the-royal-face, was considered to be enshrined in a sacred triple axe, which symbolized the three priestly families on the island, without whose aid the gods could not be acceptably worshipped. Tane-of-the-royal-face was one of the very few much-represented gods *not* surrendered to the missionaries, but hidden in caves.'

It is refreshing to read that the Cook Islanders held back at least some of their religious symbols. Unfortunately no specimen of multiple-headed adzes has survived.

Like ordinary adzes, the ceremonial ones were composed of three parts, namely haft, basalt blade, and sennit lashing. Each part of ceremonial adzes was an elaboration of utilitarian forms. The oldest adzes of religious affinity are of the most precise craftsmanship. Their handles are slender, the stone blades are delicately made (and often are wide and flat), while the helves are covered with the K-motif surface decoration applied in a restrained manner. In later times, when adzes of this type were sold as trade items, they increased in size with loss of quality but with a greater variety of handle types. In the nineteenth century, adzes were made with pedestal bases and a wide range of pierced work on the handles. The contrast between the older adzes (plate 103) and those of later date (plate 101) can be seen from the illustrations.

Peter Buck describes how he met the last 'ceremonial' adze-maker in the year 1929. Thus we can estimate that a trade in these adzes continued for over a century after the demise of traditional Mangaian religion. He writes:

'On my last visit to Mangaia in 1929, Taniera Tangitoru was the sole survivor of a succession of craftsmen who had for a century made carved adzes for the foreign markets. In the early part of the foreign production period the craftsmen no doubt adhered to stone age technique in the forms of the hafts, carving patterns, lashing

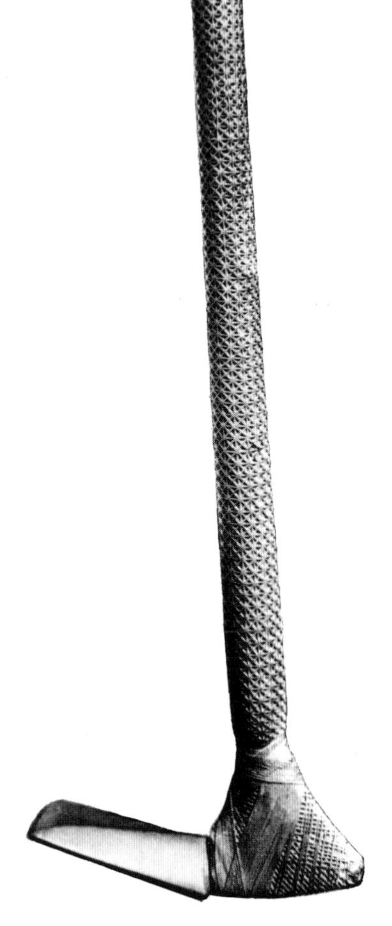

103. Ceremonial adze from Mangaia in the Cook Islands. According to museum records, this adze was collected during Captain Cook's brief contact with the Mangaians in 1777. If this is true, then it is probably the first Mangaian ceremonial adze collected. It is an ideal representative of the old form of slim helve and proportionally balanced blade held in place by beautiful sennit lashings. *Length: 24 in (61 cm). Dunedin, Otago Museum*

design, and types of adz heads used, albeit they employed steel tools on the woodwork. In the course of time, however, craftsmen without the careful training of the immediate forbears were influenced more and more by the desire to please their foreign buyers. With steel tools, changes in the shape of the hafts were readily produced, and new carving motifs were introduced to create a greater appeal to the limited market. As the production of artifacts was merely a side issue, the details of carving finish and lashing technique received less attention. The later products have cruder carving, and the lashings indicate clearly that the unique Mangaian form of the triple-triangle design had been forgotten. As the supply of adz heads appropriate to the carved hafts fell short, any available adz head was used.'

The surprising fact remains that an overall high quality prevailed in Mangaian adzes and Ra'ivavaean paddles which were made for trade. The surface decorations of both adzes and paddles are so similar that Austral paddles are often labelled 'Mangaia' and Mangaian adzes labelled 'Austral Islands' or 'Ra'ivavae'. The Mangaian adzes made for trade with passing ships, or for the rare visitors to the island, evolved a variety of handle forms ranging in size from about 18 inches (45 cm) to the gigantic size of 83½ inches (212 cm) of one specimen. The pedestal forms, which have a wide stylistic range in the design of the bases, can be compared with the drum bases of the Austral Islands, in so far as they are elaborately pierced in their lower parts and equally elaborate in surface decoration. The variety of this latter-day work, much of which is of excellent quality, may be seen in the trio of adzes illustrated (plate 101).

The ceremonial adze makers of Mangaia demonstrated skill in four areas: stone-blade manufacture, wood carving, sennit-plait fabrication, and ornamental lashing technique. To what degree this craftsmanship was specialized is unknown, but some division of labour would seem to have been necessary. Unfortunately, no one was sufficiently interested to record such information when it was available, and now the old-time craftsmen are dead. As we have seen the story is the same for the Society and Austral Islands. The art of the East Polynesian region is magnificent, but we can only judge it from the fragments that have come down to us. We can only hope that new materials will come to light and that the study of Polynesian art will progress in the years to come.

Bibliography

Travel in Polynesia

Beaglehole, J. C.: *The Journals of Captain James Cook on His Voyages of Discovery:*
Vol. 1. *The Voyage of the Endeavour, 1768–71.* Cambridge University Press, Cambridge, 1955
Vol. 2. *The Voyage of the Resolution and Adventure, 1772–75.* Cambridge University Press, Cambridge, 1961
Vol. 3. *The Voyage of the Resolution and Discovery, 1776–80.* 2 parts. Cambridge University Press, Cambridge, 1967
The Endeavour Journal of Joseph Banks, 1768–71. Angus and Robertson, Sydney, 1962

Bligh, W.: *A Voyage to the South Sea, Undertaken by Command of His Majesty, for the Purpose of Conveying the Breadfruit Tree to the West Indies, in His Majesty's Ship the Bounty. Including an Account of the Mutiny on Board the Said Ship.* 2 vols. G. Nicol, London, 1792

Hawkesworth, John, ed.: *An Account of the Voyages Undertaken by the Order of His Present Majesty for Making Discoveries in the Southern Hemisphere and Successively Performed by Commodore Byron, Captain Wallis, Captain Carteret and Captain Cook, in the Dolphin, the Swallow, and the Endeavour; Drawn Up from the Journals Which Were Kept by Several Commanders and from the Papers of Joseph Banks, Esq.* 3 vols. W. Strahan and T. Cadell, London, 1773

Accounts of Missionary Activities in East Polynesia

Ellis, Rev. W. W.: *Polynesian Researches.* 4 vols. Fisher, Son and Jackson, London, 1831

Gill, Rev. W. W.: *Jottings from the Pacific.* London, 1885

Williams, Rev. J.: *A Narrative of Missionary Enterprises in the South Sea Islands.* J. Snow, London, 1837

Art and material culture in East Polynesia

Archey, G: *The Art Forms of Polynesia.* Auckland Institute and Museum Bulletin, 4, Auckland, 1965

Buck, P. H.: *Arts and Crafts of the Cook Islands.* B. P. Bishop Museum, Bulletin 179, Honolulu, 1944

Dodge, E. S.: *The Hervey Island Adzes in the Peabody Museum of Art.* Peabody Museum, Salem, 1937

Cranstone, B. A. L. and Gowers, H. J.: 'The Tahitian Mourner's Dress' in *British Museum Quarterly,* XXXII, 3–4: 138–44, 1968

Kooijman, S.: 'Ancient Polynesian God-figures' in *Journal of the Polynesian Society,* 73: 110–25, 1964

Rose, R. G.: 'On the Origin and Diversity of "Tahitian" Janiform Fly Whisks', paper 10 in *The Art of Oceania.* McMaster University, Hamilton, Ontario, 1974

Silverthorne, H.: *Society Islands' Pounders.* B. P. Bishop Museum, Occasional papers, XI, 17, Honolulu, 1936

Ethnography

Buck, P. H.: *Mangaian Society.* B. P. Bishop Museum, Bulletin 92. Honolulu, 1934

Bellwood, P.: The Polynesians: Prehistory of an island people. London, 1978

Handy, E. S. C.: *History and Culture of the Society Islands.* B. P. Bishop Museum, Bulletin 79, Honolulu, 1930

Oliver, D. L.: *Ancient Tahitian Society.* 3 vols. University of Hawaii, Honolulu, 1974

Vérin, P.: *L'Ancienne Civilization de Rurutu.* ORSTOM, Mémoires 33, Paris, 1969

Exhibitions and Pictorial Sources

Duff, R.: *No sort of Iron: Culture of Cook's Polynesians. A Cook Bicentenary Exhibition.* Art Galleries and Museums Assoc. of New Zealand, Christchurch

Kaeppler, A. L.: *'Artificial Curiosities' An Exposition of Native Manufactures Collected on the Three Pacific Voyages of Captain James Cook, R.N.* B. P. Bishop Museum, special publication number 65, Honolulu, 1978

Phelps, S.: *Art and Artefacts of the Pacific, Africa and the Americas: The James Hooper Collection.* Hutchinson, London, 1976

Smith, B.: *European Vision and the South Pacific . . . 1768–1850.* Clarendon Press, Oxford, 1960

Acknowledgements and list of illustrations

The author and Blacker Calmann Cooper Ltd would like to thank the museums and collectors who have allowed their works to be reproduced in this book. They would also like to thank the photographers and photographic libraries who have allowed their photographs to be reproduced; in particular they would like to thank Henry Brewer of the British Museum photographic service and Gwil Owen, the photographer at the Cambridge Museum of Archaeology and Ethnology, for the help they provided.

Cover subject: Tahitian figure. British Museum, London

1. Te Po, a Rarotongan chief. Museum of Archaeology and Ethnology, Cambridge
2. A Tahitian double canoe, drawn by John Webber. British Library, London
3. Matavai Bay in Tahiti, painted by William Hodges. National Maritime Museum, Greenwich
4. Matavai Bay, drawn by William Hodges. British Museum, London
5. Man of Rurutu, a pencil and watercolour sketch by John Webber. British Library, London
6. An interior view of the temple at Atahuru, Tahiti, painted by John Webber. British Museum, London
7. Attack on Captain Wallis's ship in Matavai Bay.
8. Purea handing a palm frond to Captain Wallis.
9. Detail of paddle handle. Museum of Archaeology and Ethnology, Cambridge
10. Portrait of Omai in an engraving by Bertolozzi after a painting by Nathaniel Dance Holland. Museum of Archaeology and Ethnology, Cambridge

11 and 12. Two views of the Taputapuatea *marae* on Ra'iatea. Photo Axel Poignant

13 and 14. Companion pictures from *Life in the Southern Isles* by the Rev. W. W. Gill. Museum of Archaeology and Ethnology, Cambridge

15. People of Rarotonga delivering their god images to missionaries, from *Missionary Enterprises* by the Rev. J. Williams. Museum of Archaeology and Ethnology, Cambridge
16. Tahitian wooden figure. British Museum, London
17. Tahitian wooden figure illustrated in plate 16, with Tahitian wreath. Photo Haddon Collection, Cambridge
18. King Pomare I, by William Hodges. National Library of Australia, Canberra
19. A Dance in Otaheiti, an engraving after a sketch by John Webber. British Library, London
20. Two bamboo nose flutes. Museum of Archaeology and Ethnology, Cambridge
21. Groups of Tahitian artifacts, drawn by J. F. Miller. British Library, London

Index

Page numbers in *italic* refer to the illustrations and their captions